2 ||
8·69

the
animals

came

dancing

the animals

came

dancing

howard l. harrod

native american
sacred ecology
and animal kinship

the university of arizona press
tucson

First printing

The University of Arizona Press

© 2000 The Arizona Board of Regents

All rights reserved

♾ This book is printed on acid-free, archival-
quality paper.

Manufactured in the United States of America

05 04 03 02 01 00 6 5 4 3 2 1

Library of Congress Cataloging-in-Publication
Data

Harrod, Howard L.

The animals came dancing: Native American
sacred ecology and animal kinship / Howard L.
Harrod

p.   cm.

Includes bibliographical references and index.

ISBN 0-8165-2026-7 (cloth: alk. paper)

ISBN 0-8165-2027-5 (pbk.: alk. paper)

1. Indians of North America—Hunting—
Great Plains.   2. Indians of North America—
Great Plains—Religion.   3. Human-animal
relationships—Great Plains.   4. Siksika
Indians—Hunting.   5. Siksika Indians—
Religion.   I. Title.

E78.G73 H353 2000   99-6771

799.2978–dc21   CIP

British Library Cataloguing-in-Publication Data
A catalogue record for this book is available
from the British Library.

for Annemarie

We need another and a wiser and perhaps a more mystical concept of animals. Remote from universal nature, and living by complicated artifice, man in civilization surveys the creature through the glass of his knowledge and sees thereby a feather magnified and the whole image in distortion. We patronize them for their incompleteness, for their tragic fate of having taken form so far below ourselves. And therein we err, and greatly err. For the animal shall not be measured by man. In a world older and more complete than ours they move finished and complete, gifted with extensions of the senses we have lost or never attained, living by voices we shall never hear. They are not our brethren, they are not our underlings; they are other nations, caught with ourselves in the net of life and time, fellow prisoners of the splendor and travail of the earth.

—Henry Beston, *The Outermost House*

contents

preface

While reading "A Study of Siouan Cults," written by James O. Dorsey, I came across a passage that lured me, haunted me, and finally motivated me to write this book. The text that invaded my consciousness was an old Hidatsa tradition that portrayed a female figure known as Grandmother. This primordial being gave the Hidatsas two kettles that were used in a ritual that probably focused on both agriculture and hunting. The oral tradition, embodied in songs and dances, recalled not only the time of the Grandmother but also the fecundity of primal waters: "She directed the ancestors of the present Indians to preserve the kettles and to remember the great waters, *whence came all the animals dancing*" (Dorsey 1894: 513, my emphasis).

"The animals came dancing"—this phrase condensed many meanings that surrounded Northern Plains animal rituals I had studied. When a person who is not a hunter begins to write a book on Northern Plains hunting rituals, however, obstacles soon appear. I could not overcome some of the barriers, such as being culturally non-Indian, but I addressed my experiential difficulties in part by living and writing, as often as possible, near the Northern Plains, where buffalo hunting was a way of life for Native American peoples.

There are also deep ironies that rise up in experience as one seeks to reimagine this past. For example, much of the research took place in a forested valley in northwestern Montana. This valley lies on the western border of Glacier National Park. On the park's eastern boundary, foothills abruptly give way to the vast expanse of the plains and to the Blackfoot homeland. It is ironic that the plains comprising the Blackfeet Reservation are lacking in buffalo, except for a few animals here and there, while the valley where I write is one of the last places in the lower forty-eight where animals that were here during the nineteenth century still exist in predator-prey relationships. Grizzly and black bears; wolves, coyotes, and mountain lions; whitetail and mule deer; as well as elk and moose dwell in and seasonally move through this valley. Smaller animals such as wolverines, porcupines, snowshoe hares, and badgers also occupy the land. And there are of course the great raptor birds that engaged the symbolic imagination of Native American people: eagles and ospreys—and always, ravens.

Another irony is that, though I am not a hunter, part of my research took place during hunting season. Superimposed upon hunting done by animal predators was the human hunter-predator, mostly male and almost always of European descent. Contemporary Indian hunters were also about, but they were not visible in this valley. I have never seen an African American hunter in this place. The human hunters who were of European heritage had been socialized in cultural values and practices that are significantly different from those of their predecessors among Northern Plains hunters.

Modern non-Indian hunters, at least in northwestern Montana, are immersed in a hunting tradition with multiple roots. For some, hunting is a family tradition that is passed on from father to sons and sometimes daughters as well. For others, hunting is not mediated by a family tradition but is acquired through internalizing values that surround sport, the outdoors, and the recreation industry. These people often acquire proficiency with weapons through institutionalized training rather than from their fathers or mothers;

and while their hunting skills are honed through practice, this practice often takes place under the watchful eye of an outfitter in a hunting camp.

While many local hunters know the land, there are increasingly larger numbers of hunters who come from out of state, paying large fees for their licenses. Unlike local hunters who use the area, these people possess only superficial knowledge about its character and history. They come to kill animals, and as with some local hunters, this activity provides them with a supplemental source of food. None of these hunters, whether local or from other states, depend exclusively upon hunting for their basic subsistence. Even so, some of the local hunters do hunt in a manner that reflects their sensibility that spiritual meanings surround the killing of animals for food. For example, one hunter said, "My quality of life would be severely compromised if I could not continue the hunt. My spirituality would also suffer. My cabin is full of skulls and dead things to remind me every day of the death I have brought to these animals. Every day I honor these animals. I want them 'in my face' so as not to forget" (Lee Secrest, personal correspondence).

Contemporary hunters are also aware, though sometimes dimly, of the ritual aspects that infuse their activities. These ritual dimensions revolve around the handling of weapons and ammunition as well as the manipulation of increasingly sophisticated gear, such as devices that reproduce animal calls. Special language surrounds hunting activities, and distinctive clothing marks off the hunter from other human companions. Camouflaged, the bow hunter melts into the surrounding larch and lodgepole forests, while the gun hunter announces his or her presence with brightly colored orange.

Modern non-Indian hunters are also aware that their behavior is restrained by law and, more informally, by shared taboos surrounding the killing of animals. Shooting from a vehicle, poaching on private or public land, hunting out of season or without a proper license, and wanton killing or brutalizing of animals are all illegal. In some cases such behavior is also restrained by norms that function as taboos and may provide a more powerful check on hunting behavior than does fear of the law embodied in the person of a game warden.

There are loose analogies that can be drawn between modern hunting and the hunting of Native American predecessors, but in the end these analogies point up what are only shadow similarities. The values that informed hunting in the cultures of Northern Plains peoples were embedded in ritual processes and understandings of animals that were very different from those that shape the behavior and understanding of most modern hunters.

Northern Plains hunters were introduced as children (usually male) to the shared traditions that surrounded killing animals for food. Oral memories were rich with examples of how animals gave their bodies to the people, often agreeing to become food because they had established kinship relations with humans. These traditions and their associated skills were mediated to children and youth through extended families and were embodied in examples of good hunters, usually provided by male relatives, and bad hunters, often mediated through narratives about Trickster's foolish hunting behavior. Unlike the modern hunter, the continued survival of the group, or at least the extended family, depended upon the bounty that flowed from successful hunting.

Plains peoples also created ritual processes that surrounded their weapons and, after they acquired horses, included these animals as well. They used special animal-calling rituals to guarantee success on the hunt, and they employed rituals of renewal to insure that the animals would always return. Sometimes esoteric language and specialized shamanic roles accompanied their hunting rituals. And Plains hunters employed body paints and special dress in the rituals that were enacted before and sometimes after hunting.

While not backed by law in the sense that modern restraints on hunting behavior are, Northern Plains hunters learned the appropriate taboos and sought diligently to embody them. There were consequences that followed from the violation of these rules. If powerful nonhuman persons, such as animal masters, were offended, they could withhold the game. If the animals themselves were offended, they could refuse to give themselves to the hunters. In the world of Northern Plains hunters, game animals possessed an acute awareness, personal qualities, and refined sensitivities. They could and would withhold themselves from the careless or disrespectful hunter.

There is another set of experiences that deepened my understanding of important aspects of Northern Plains hunting. During the fall and early winter of 1993, my friend Lee Secrest taught me some of the rudimentary principles involved in tanning the skins of wild animals. Lee is one of the handful of individuals in the United States who employ the process of brain tanning, a very old technique that was used among Northern Plains peoples. In addition, Lee is a talented artist who has produced creative interpretations inspired by the tradition of North American Indian hide painting.

The products of Lee's artistic labors as a hide painter are not only aesthetically satisfying, they also shimmer with the power and presence of the animals he represents on the hide's surface. Likewise, the products of his work as a brain tanner are of such high quality and so beautiful that they are in great demand. Some of his finished hides were used in making clothing for movies such as *Dances with Wolves* and *Thunderheart*. Most impressive is the fact that one of his painted hides is now on display in the Smithsonian Institution.

During part of the winter of 1993, I was privileged to work on a bison hide under Lee Secrest's expert supervision. I experienced the smell and felt the texture of the animal's skin. This encounter provided me with a palpable connection to the animal from which the skin had been taken. While Lee has often told me that I will never understand Northern Plains hunters until I kill a large animal, working on this bison hide surely moved me closer toward such understanding, even though I will probably never hunt. So if there is a sense of connection to animals and hunting that comes through in the book, it is largely dependent upon the effects of these powerful experiences upon me.

As I look out on the main range of the Rocky Mountains in winter, I am moved not only by their fierce snow-covered splendor but also by the thought that contexts such as these may become more and more marginal to the experience of future humans. As the buffalo on the Northern Plains were almost driven to extinction in the nineteenth century, so much of the twentieth century has threatened the delicate balance between humans and animals in North America and elsewhere in the world. Human activities, summarized by the term "development," spread themselves over increasingly larger areas, and as the animals retreat (or come into conflict with humans), there is less and less habitat for them to occupy.

Hunters on the Northern Plains lived within rather than against their surrounding environments. Their relationship to animal beings was so informed by religious meanings that it constituted a sacred ecology that may not be completely recoverable, either by their successors or by the wider non-Indian population. The term "sacred ecology" refers to the sensibility, evident in Northern Plains cultures, that the world was constituted by powers that took the form of Persons. In hunting cultures, these Persons often appeared in animal form.

My hope is that an imaginative entry into the sacred ecology of Northern Plains societies will expand the discussion about how wild animals and the natural contexts that support them can be preserved and extended into the future. And, most important, I hope to contribute to the broader process of reimagining our relationships with the nonhuman world. Being affected by Northern Plains animal rituals may help shape attitudes and behaviors that will preserve wild animals and enable us to give this precious gift to future generations. On rare occasions, the shadowy image of future generations stands out powerfully and clearly in our imagination, and sometimes, like the mountains and the animals, these distant others may speak. As we enter the twenty-first century, it is up to us to listen.

acknowledgments

I would like to thank Vanderbilt University for supporting my research over the past thirty years. That support, especially in the form of fellowships and sabbatical leaves, has created the space for me to travel, write, and spend time on the Northern Plains. Three colleagues at Vanderbilt, Doug Knight, Sallie McFague, and Eugene TeSelle, have read the manuscript in various stages, and I thank them for their respective efforts. Sally Smith Holt deserves a special thanks for her work on the index, as do Nancy Weatherwax for her careful proofreading and Mary M. Hill for her excellent copyediting of the manuscript. I am also grateful for the insight and tolerance provided by several generations of students, especially those in my Native American religions classes and my seminars on animal rituals, where some of these ideas were first presented. Research without students to teach is, in my view, always incomplete.

Much of the work on this book took place in northwestern Montana, and the support of several persons was essential to bring it to fruition. Donna and Tom Marx as well as Nancy and John Hubble have been more than friends, and they know how much I appreciate their extended family sensibilities. In addition, Nancy Hubble has long been interested in the work of George Bird Grinnell and has generously shared both her knowledge and her manuscript collection. Lee Secrest and Amy Edmonds also provided essential insights into the values and dispositions of contemporary hunters. Lee's long residence in northwestern Montana and Amy's expertise in wildlife biology have greatly improved my understanding of animals and hunting.

My longest associations with Indian people have been on the Blackfeet Reservation, which lies in northwestern Montana to the east of Glacier National Park. I am particularly grateful for my friendship with Long Standing Bear Chief of Browning, Montana. He has provided me with linguistic and cultural insights that would have been impossible to acquire by any other means.

The staff of the University of Arizona Press, especially Christine Szuter and Alan M. Schroder, have been supportive of this project as well as my other books that have been published there. They do good work, and I thank them.

Finally, I would like to thank Annemarie, who is my companion and best friend. This work is dedicated to her.

animals

and
cultural

values

Human experiences of other living beings in their environment are shaped by distinct culture patterns. These patterns are encoded in a people's language, appearing concretely in the naming of the nonhuman beings that are a part of particular ecosystems. The naming of animals gives rise to a complex set of cultural categories that both constitutes a sense of difference and establishes various forms of relationships between humans and animals. Such categories also project particular forms of relationships within animal groups, such as understandings of predator and prey interactions.

Naming animals is part of a larger process of world construction that gives rise to a shared complex of cultural objects and experiences. The stabilization of a particular world picture makes possible the transmission of that portrait and its corresponding attitudes, values, and experiences to future generations; in short, a society becomes possible. Once this occurs and perceptions of particular aspects of the world, such as in the case of animals, are routinized, then these beings may become essential features of the dreams, imaginings, and literary or oral traditions of a people.[1]

There are obvious differences among cultures with respect to the naming and experience of animals, as well as other living nonhuman aspects of their worlds. There are also differences that develop within cultures as a consequence of particular historical development. For example, changes in basic categories, such as those concerning animals, may emerge either when groups come into initial contact with one another or when one group conquers another group. The cultural crises that are created by contact, and always by conquest, are crises of meaning as one world picture is delegitimated in favor of another. The suffering that proceeds from these crises—especially the processes of colonization and conquest—involves deep anguish that flows from assaults on human bodies by disease and warfare as well as assaults on the social world as previously taken-for-granted patterns of economic, religious, and kinship relations are severely strained or collapse altogether. And when human beings are killed, especially in great numbers, the meanings that constitute their shared social world may be severely undermined or even destroyed. The process of conquest or colonization may never be complete in the sense that particular cultural meanings are completely obliterated. For example, many of the historical values, attitudes, and culture patterns may be glimpsed, often creatively altered or transformed, in the behaviors of contemporary Indian people.

Reconstructing Cultural Meanings

I am particularly interested in recovering a sense of the understanding that hunting peoples on the Northern Plains had of the animals upon which they depended for food and other products. I am further interested in the culture patterns that produced significant continuities in their experience of animals. As this study proceeds, it will become clear that these cultural continuities were maintained by shared symbols enacted in ritual processes. Thus the study focuses particularly upon *religion,* which essentially has to do with those realities that people experience as transcendent sources not only of meaning but also of life and their present world context.

My focus is upon cultural meanings and shared social worlds that flourished during a particular time period, roughly 1750–1850, and my description will range over groups living mainly on the Northern Plains. The description of cultural meanings involves mining the memories of Native Americans who lived during the last part of the nineteenth century and the early decades of the twentieth. These memories were recorded by anthropologists and other observers. The texts produced by that process exhibit all of the problems that come with the translation of oral traditions into written form: the problems of competence or lack of facility in Indian languages and their translation into English; the cultural interests and prejudices of the European observers; the tendency to decontextualize cultural meanings; and the suffering endured by Indian people as the buffalo were destroyed and their indigenous ways were dramatically altered with the emergence of reservation life.[2]

A student of these traditions soon learns, however, that the memories of Native peoples, even though recorded under difficult and even exploitative conditions, often exhibit an amazing consistency and tenacity. These memories sometimes connect to traditions that may be deeper than the time frame of this study. For example, those who were alive in 1910 and who were sixty years old were born in 1850. These people lived during the last stages of buffalo days and learned the traditions of their parents, who, if they were thirty years old in 1850, would have been born in 1820. If the grandparents were alive in 1820 and they happened to be sixty years old or older, they would have been born in the 1750s or 1760s. It is evident that the chain of memory and transmission of oral traditions could be even older, involving the experiences of great-grandparents.

This does not mean, of course, that these traditions were impervious to change. That was certainly not the case. Rather, oral traditions exhibited both tenacity and continuity while at the same time maintaining the flexibility and dynamism to expand or contract as circumstances required. The creative possibilities for innovation were quite evident on the Northern Plains as wave after wave of people from different cultural backgrounds migrated into the area at different points in time.

What is sedimented in the ethnographies of the late nineteenth and early twentieth centuries, then, are oral traditions that have been reduced to texts.

animals and cultural values

They are imperfect, often appearing as fragments that bear traces of cultural contact with missionaries and other Europeans. They are mediated through the alien linguistic and interpretive frames of European observers. And they have the quality of being frozen in time, especially because oral traditions of present Native American peoples continue and often motivate processes of contemporary cultural renewal. Such cultural renewal exhibits both continuities and discontinuities with memories of the past. Nevertheless, these early memories, captured in texts, provide a rich resource for reconstructing a portrait of past cultural meanings.

Animals in Contemporary Popular Culture

In order to understand and appreciate the hunting cultures and the shared social worlds that emerged on the Northern Plains, contemporary Euro-Americans need to reflect deeply on the elements of their own taken-for-granted view of animals as well as the other living beings in their environment. If these views are brought to the surface of awareness and examined closely, then the contrasting Northern Plains understanding of animals will become much clearer.

One of the problematical features of any such interpretive attempt has to do with the fundamental influence of powerful forms of scientific thought that shape Euro-American perceptions and experience of animals. While it would be fruitful to attend to descriptions of animals that are found in wildlife biology, as well as in studies of the history of animal taxonomies, the analysis that follows is not focused specifically upon these systems of knowledge. While such knowledge directly or indirectly informs our interpretations, the focus instead is upon images of animals that are constituted in and mediated by popular culture.

One of the dimensions of Euro-American popular culture that profoundly shapes the experience of animals is a value complex that has been nourished by particular religious traditions. Some popular Christian understandings of the creation narratives that appear in the Hebrew Bible, for example, have led to the view that animals were provided by God strictly for the use of human beings.[3] Moreover, according to this view, the First Man was given "dominion" over the animals and was commissioned to name them.[4] These popular religious understandings were often combined with Enlightenment traditions concerning the nature of rationality that drew a fundamental distinction between humans and animals. In this view animals were "dumb," lacking speech and thus the superior form of rationality possessed by human beings. As a consequence, humans were placed at the top of a hierarchy of being that clearly ranked animals in a lower, subordinate position.[5]

A particularly pervasive value complex that took up some of these themes and deeply formed the North American ethos derived from the utilitarian philosophy that arose in England during the eighteenth and nineteenth centuries.[6] The part of that view that has become deeply woven into the American ethos and that is especially important to bring into awareness is the notion that the value of things is essentially determined by their utility. Things are "good for" some other end, and the most desired end has to do with the production of good consequences for those who use them and finally for the greatest good for the greatest number. From this perspective, the value of animals lies in the use to which they can be put, especially as they contribute to the service of human needs. Human needs can be understood on a continuum from the most basic biological requirements for food to the aesthetic impulses that lead to the contemplation of nature and animals.

The classical utilitarian motifs that shape the American ethos and give rise to particular experiences of animals are complicated by another set of images in popular culture. These images and their implied value structures are deeply rooted in an older folklore about animals, such as the stories produced by the Grimm brothers and the portraits that appear in the Uncle Remus cycle. A casual perusal of contemporary children's books, at both the level of image and text, reveals striking continuities with the older folklore; in addition, reprints of the earlier literature are also readily available. In these traditions animals speak, they have distinct personalities, they engage in purposeful action, and they relate to humans in particular ways. These cultural images have structured the imagination and experience of countless generations of North American children. Some of these images surely remain deeply embedded in the consciousness of the adults who as children were exposed to them.

Interacting with text and representations in books are a plethora of three-dimensional animal toys that evoke forms of interaction in children's play

animals and cultural values

that are not possible through reading and pictorial imagery. Children name these animals, create play worlds that they occupy, sleep with them, and imbue them with distinct personality traits. Like the animals in folktales, these three-dimensional toys exhibit purposeful actions that often form important aspects of the child's subjective experience and contribute to the construction of his or her world.

If these toy animals are understood against the cultural context that includes not only folktales and modern children's books but also the powerful representations in television and movies, then the portrait we are drawing becomes even more complex. The sophisticated animals of *Sesame Street* join the host of animals portrayed in Walt Disney movies and cartoons to produce an almost overwhelming set of animal images to which many if not almost all North American children are regularly exposed. Given the wide diffusion of television and movies around the world, this exposure has now become global in its scope. Movies like *The Lion King* contribute only the latest layer of animal symbolism to a long and complex popular tradition.

The projection of animals that populate folklore and the visual media prepares children to experience living animals in the contexts that North American culture readily provides: pet animals, domestic animals (an experience more widespread in rural as compared with urban contexts), and zoo animals. Encounters with "wild" animals are very limited and virtually nonexistent for most North American children. The encounters that do occur sometimes lead to tragic consequences as, for example, when children become victims of an animal attack in one of the nation's national parks. Even though such attacks are rare, they often receive a great deal of attention in both the print and television media.

As the play worlds of children give way to the life worlds of adults, the themes developed in the older folklore, modern stories, and media imagery constitute a deeply sedimented, taken-for-granted foundation for experiences of animals that are intimately connected with powerful social values and correspondingly influential social structures. Of particular interest here is the massive recreation industry and its pervasive infrastructure. Animals are projected in this industry either as exotic occupants of national parks, ready to provide the sensitive tourist with a unique aesthetic experience, or as "sport" animals whose existence provides enjoyment for recreational hunters.

In the first case, the tourist is enticed to experience the natural contexts of the national park system as a series of zoolike enclosures where animals may be observed and enjoyed by humans. Those seeking such recreational experiences often feel deprived and even angered if animals in the parks do not offer themselves as objects of the touristic experience.[7] In the second case, the vast hunting and fishing industries portray animals as objects of sport and recreation. The infrastructure of these industries—sport hunting organizations, hunting and fishing programs on television, and the distributors of sporting equipment—seeks to inculcate in the young the practices and values associated with a particular sport.

In both of these instances the living animals and their "wild" contexts are portrayed through a cultural symbolism that renders animals as cultural artifacts, useful for human aesthetic or recreational needs. Such animals become "stock" to be managed within the parks and national forests, and they are to be "harvested" by hunting and fishing at appropriate times and in accord with certain established regulations. It is at this point that the connections with the themes of classical utilitarianism become very clear in the ethos of North American culture.

Recent debates about the reintroduction of wolves into Yellowstone Park as well as the discussions of killing possibly brucellosis-infected buffalo when they range outside the park are ready examples of conflicts generated against the background of a human-centered utilitarianism. These debates take on an ironic dimension because both sides in the discussion often ground their arguments in a utilitarian paradigm. Cattle and sheep ranchers argue that the reintroduction of wolves will lead to killing of their animals (a "bad" consequence), while environmental groups may argue that wolf recovery in the West will lead to a restoration of predator-prey relations that pertained in the nineteenth century (a "good" consequence).

Implied in the foregoing analysis is the notion that modern cultural values and social processes have alienated most contemporary Euro-Americans from the experience of animals in "wild" contexts, meaning the contexts that still possess relative autonomy in relation to the cultural pressures mentioned earlier.[8] It is true, of course, that such contexts have rapidly diminished around the world and exist only in very small areas within the continental United States. It is also true that the term "alienation" is descriptive of a condition that is not often clearly experienced but that instead lurks at the edges of consciousness as a vaguely disturbing reality. Certainly persons who hunt and fish as well as visit national parks experience animals, but it is the quality and character of that experience that has been questioned in this initial description.

The structural alienation from animals that characterizes the experience of many contemporary North Americans, no matter what their communities of origin, appears perhaps most clearly in the production and consumption of food. Especially in urban centers, many generations of children have matured into adulthood without any primary experience of domestic animals and no practical knowledge of where food products such as milk or eggs originate; they have seen neither milking nor egg laying. Even further from the experience of such persons is the reality of slaughtering animals for food. Nutrition and food consumption are understood more in terms of vitamins, calorie intake, and fat content. The living animal as well as the blood, entrails, and hair out of which meat products emerge are matters far from the consciousness and practical experience of most people, especially those who live completely within the web of an urban culture.

What this means is that many modern people have lost a sense of relationship to the living sources, both plant and animal, of their food supply. The cultural processes of naming plant and animal sources of food depend on structures of meaning that have been created by advertising, agribusinesses, and food distributors. Words such as "meat," "milk," "carrots," and "lettuce" derive their meaning from images projected in supermarket advertisements and are almost totally disconnected from meanings that might derive from their natural contexts. Indeed, many of these natural contexts are disappearing as food producers increasingly engage in genetic manipulation of plants and animals, as well as in the creation of highly controlled contexts for the growth and production of food "products." Increasingly larger and larger dimensions of what was once the natural world have become cultural artifacts and are now made available for large-scale manipulation and exploitation. The recent developments in animal cloning are only the latest examples of a long process of manipulation of animals, plants, and their surrounding environments, mainly for the sake of food production, but in this case also having implications for the development of other things that might be "useful" for human flourishing.

Reimagining Animals

All of these factors make for a distinctively modern world picture. A sense of distance from food sources as well as a lack of ritual performance in relationship to them are characteristic features of much contemporary human experience. When we look back in time to the experience of Native American hunting cultures on the Northern Plains, the interpretive gaps are significant. In order to approach some understanding of these peoples and their worlds, Euro-Americans must seek to strip away some of the deeply taken-for-granted cultural attitudes, values, and behaviors that have been alluded to in the previous cultural sketch. When we deconstruct these accepted images, then there is the possibility that the outlines of Northern Plains apprehensions of the nonhuman world will come more clearly into view.

My hope is that insight into this alternative view will evoke radical questions concerning present Euro-American relationships with the natural world. My desire is to uncover and give voice to what I believe is a hunger among many contemporary people for a recovery of ritual relationships between humans and the natural sources of their lives—plants, animals, and the earth itself. Whether such critical reflection will lead to a more complex understanding of human relations with nonhuman life forms and whether such a vision could lead to the construction of symbolic forms and ritual processes that would deeply reshape Euro-American experiences of the natural world are questions that are beyond the capacity of this analysis to address. But they are, nevertheless, questions that have deeply motivated the interpretation and that are absolutely essential to address. If they are not addressed, then all of us—Native Americans, African Americans, Asian Americans, Hispanic Americans, and Euro-Americans—will find ourselves living in a symbolically diminished, more lonely world.

the animals came dancing

northern **plains** · 1

hunters

Most people who have spent any time on the Great Plains recognize this word picture drawn by Scott Momaday:

> The earth unfolds and the limit of the land recedes. Clusters of trees, and animals grazing far in the distance, cause the vision to reach away and wonder to build upon the mind. The sun follows a longer course in the day, and the sky is immense beyond all comparison. The great billowing clouds that sail upon it are shadows that move upon the grain like water, dividing the light. . . . The sun is at home on the plains. (Momaday 1969; quoted in Kehoe 1981: 272)

The Northern Plains are characterized by just such striking scenes, as well as by an extreme and often unforgiving climate. Temperatures well above one hundred degrees Fahrenheit are common in summer, and blowing snow, subzero temperatures, and wind chill factors as much as fifty degrees or more below zero are common in winter. Warmer chinook winds moving down the eastern slopes of the Rocky Mountain front provide occasional and often surprising breaks in the grip that winter usually has on the land. Even though rainfall amounts are small on the Northern Plains and stands of trees are found mostly along the streams and rivers, spectacular thunderstorms and drenching showers relieve both humans and animals during spring and summer. Snow packs that build up along the spine of the Rocky Mountains melt during spring and early summer, providing the streams and rivers with rushing supplies of fresh water and occasionally bringing floods that rage violently through the countryside.

Even now, animal life is still abundant compared to other areas, and some of the great mammals that lived in earlier times on the Northern Plains and were hunted by pre-Columbian Native Americans still occupy this habitat, thanks in part to the protection afforded by the Endangered Species Act. Whitetail and mule deer, elk, moose, mountain lions, wolves, black bears, and grizzly bears all have viable populations in this region. Bald and golden eagles as well as osprey are regularly to be seen fishing the rivers. Herds of buffalo may presently be found in Yellowstone National Park and at the National Bison Range near Moise, Montana, and private herds exist both in Montana and South Dakota. As many as sixty million animals are estimated to have lived on the Great Plains at the dawn of the nineteenth century, providing the Northern Plains peoples with a material abundance that began its disastrous and final decline by the middle of that century.

While there have been attempts to give precise and technical definitions of the Northern Plains boundaries (Ewers 1967; Wissler 1908), a rougher approximation will suffice for this study. The area of interest is bounded on the west by the Rocky Mountains and the Continental Divide, reaching north to the southern portions of Alberta and Saskatchewan in Canada; the southern border is unclear but for this study extends no farther than the Platte River in Nebraska. The eastern border is formed by the Missouri River. This area includes Montana and Wyoming east of the Rocky Mountains and the Continental Divide, the parts of Canada already mentioned, the western portions of North and South Dakota, and northern Nebraska.

This study deals mainly with twelve Northern Plains groups that belonged to three broad language families. Algonquian speakers include the three divisions of the Blackfeet (the Piegans, Bloods, and Siksikas, or Northern Blackfeet)

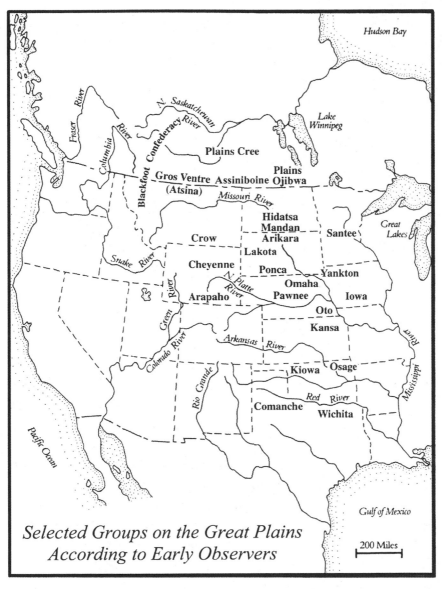

Selected Groups on the Great Plains According to Early Observers

(Drawn by Dominic M. Doyle)

and their allies the Atsinas, as well as the Cheyennes, Arapahoes, and Western Crees. Siouan groups include the Lakotas, Assiniboines, Mandans, Hidatsas, and Crows, and Caddoan speakers include the Arikaras and Pawnees. The people who became known as the Crows had separated from the Hidatsas, and the Arikaras were an offshoot of the Pawnees. Some of these people were more recent occupants of the Northern Plains, while others were more ancient inhabitants.[1]

Predecessors of the Pawnees, Arikaras, Mandans, and perhaps some of the Hidatsas had occupied the area of the Missouri River and its tributaries beginning perhaps as early as 1100 C.E. They lived in earth lodges and developed economies based on both agriculture and hunting. The expansion of the fur trade in the eighteenth century and population pressures from the east were probably contributing factors, along with the spread of guns, that stimulated migrations of numerous peoples into the Northern Plains. Siouan peoples were a part of this great migration, the Lakotas representing the most western edge, and Algonquians such as the Blackfeet, Crees, Cheyennes, and Arapahoes made their way into the area, the Blackfeet being perhaps among the earliest arrivals. These peoples had come from different homelands and cultural backgrounds, and they became, with the arrival of the horse in the eighteenth century, the "typical" Plains buffalo hunters so prominent in the popular American imagination.[2]

Understanding the meanings that surrounded the hunting of animals in Northern Plains societies requires that we reconstruct some view of that part of their everyday world. Hunting animals was an essential activity, providing the people not only with supplies of meat but also skins for lodges, clothing, and household items. Hunting was deeply motivated by the need for these products and was informed by shared systems of knowledge that had been passed down from generation to generation. These systems of knowledge had to do with the behavior of animals and their relation to particular habitats as well as knowledge about how to hunt and kill them successfully. The people also had extensive knowledge about how to process the products of the hunt and how to store food for future use.

Hunting was more than simply a necessary "economic activity" as most contemporary people would understand that phrase. The hunting project was not only informed by traditional knowledge, shared practices, and learned skills, it was also fundamentally interrelated with religious symbols and ritual processes. Hunting was grounded in symbolic meanings that derived from shared religious traditions that gave shape to more specific hunting rituals. These traditions were as much a part of the hunter's everyday world as were the other aspects of skill and knowledge that were brought to bear on this important activity. Some of the religious meanings that surrounded hunting are alluded to in this chapter, but the remainder of the book provides an extensive analysis of hunting rituals and their symbolic forms.

Imagining the everyday world of Northern Plains hunters is difficult for many contemporaries. Popular images of Indians mediated by paintings such as those by George Catlin, photographs such as those produced by Edward S. Curtis, novels such as Ruth Beebee Hill's *Hanta Yo* (1979), and movies such as Kevin Costner's *Dances with Wolves* (1990) are very powerful. They have given rise to a popular symbolic layer that is almost impenetrable. Encounters with Native American peoples in the present are shaped—and mis-shaped—by these images, and efforts to understand the past are often consciously or unconsciously controlled by this interpretive horizon.

Fortunately there are descriptions that may be used to construct a more realistic vision of Native American hunting on the Northern Plains. The most important of these descriptions come from memories of Native American people that were recorded by anthropologists, fur traders, missionaries, and other non-Indian observers. Even though these materials do not preserve all of the dynamic forms of the oral traditions they seek to document, and they are flawed by the interests and perspectives of the observers, they are still invaluable sources for evoking a sense of everyday life. In this sense, these descriptions are primary for our understanding. Observations of Europeans who either lived among or visited Northern Plains groups supplement Native American memories in many instances. Archaeological investigations provide some limited, though valuable, insights into the historical depth of the hunting practices that were characteristic of people observed in the eighteenth and nineteenth centuries. All three types of literature are used in this chapter.

Fortunately the experience of a particular group can be used to typify the hunting activities of many peoples on the Northern Plains because hunting practices and food production techniques were highly routinized. The religious meanings surrounding some of these activities also assumed typical form, but at this level there was considerable variation in symbolic content among Northern Plains peoples. The Blackfoot experience will provide us with an initial portrait of hunting and food production that may be generalized to other groups; the remaining chapters explore the rich differences that characterized the religious understandings that surrounded food sources among various groups.

From June until September 1911 a number of Blackfoot oral traditions were recorded by a Dutch linguist, C. C. Uhlenbeck (1913). Even though Uhlenbeck was a student of the Blackfoot language, these materials could not have been produced without the work of Joseph Tatsey. A member of the Piegan division of the Blackfeet, Tatsey lived on the Blackfeet Reservation in Montana. He provided Uhlenbeck with an English rendering of most of the oral traditions recorded during this period; in addition, he provided essential assistance in the process of transliteration by repeating the traditions in Blackfoot so that they could be recorded as texts.

One text painted a word picture of aspects of everyday life as it was remembered by a Piegan named Blood. This narrative began with memories that Blood had received from his family as well as his contemporaries concerning "how the ancient Piegans moved about, how they ate, the things they cooked with, the things they had happy times with, how they fought in war, how they played, and how they dressed, the way I heard about them" (Uhlenbeck 1913: 1).

These memories were tied together in a narrative that included two distinct layers. The first layer described Blackfoot hunting during the period after they acquired horses and guns in the last quarter of the eighteenth century; although Blood was not entirely clear on this point, hunting with horses included some limited use of guns as well as a continued reliance on the bow and arrow. The second layer contained memories of a time before the Blackfeet had horses. At this earlier time they hunted buffalo on foot and used dogs to carry their belongings. These memories represented layers of the oral tradition that were understood to be true but that transcended Blood's experience.

These aspects of the narrative were mediated to him in the form of shared understandings of how things were in that earlier time. In that time, Blood said, "There were buffalo killed in the fall of the year. Stones were their pots. From these they got their food. Bones were their scrapers. Sticks [and] stones were things they [also] scraped with. Their arrow-points were stones, they were flint. There were no horses. They packed their lodges on dogs" (Uhlenbeck 1913: 37). Other groups who entered the Northern Plains before the horse could also be characterized by this description.

In another text narrated by Blood there was a description of buffalo hunting that also typified these activities among many different groups on the Northern Plains (Uhlenbeck 1913: 38–41). This description portrayed the people building a buffalo corral at the base of a cliff. This corral was constructed of heavy logs and was built high enough so that the animals could not escape. The drive path was marked by piles of stones forming two lines shaped like an open-ended **V**, the narrowest part of which ended at the edge of the cliff. Often the drive path was curved so that the animals could not see the edge of the cliff until it was too late for them to turn. The drive lines themselves could extend as far back as two miles from the edge of the cliff. Blood said of the Blackfeet during that time, "Those were the people, [that] were always corralling. From that they got plenty to eat" (Uhlenbeck 1913: 37).

Whether or not a corral was built at the base of the drop-off seemed to depend upon the height of the cliff. If the drive lines led to a sheer precipice, there was no need for a corral since the animals would either be killed or so severely injured that there was no chance they would escape. Another consideration is also relevant here: the number of animals that were being hunted (Frison 1978: 229–30). Large herds of animals could successfully be driven over high cliffs, whereas a smaller group of animals was very difficult to kill in this manner. Smaller groups of buffalo could more easily be driven into an arroyo or into a corral built on relatively level ground, although there are clear examples of driving larger numbers of animals into corrals as well.

Driving buffalo over cliffs or into corrals built at the base of a drop-off that was not high enough to be lethal was practiced in areas of the Northern Plains where such landforms were plentiful. In other sorts of terrain, additional methods were used, such as driving animals into a cul-de-sac or into a corral that was constructed on relatively level ground. The Siksikas, or Northern Blackfeet, lived in Alberta and, along with the Crees, built such structures. These corrals featured a log causeway over which animals were driven into the entrance of the enclosure. As they reached the entrance the animals were forced to jump down into the corral, and logs were quickly put in place to prevent their escape (Grinnell 1962: 230–31).

The buffalo corrals built by the Blackfeet had walls as high as seven or eight feet and varied in size. In 1772 a Hudson's Bay Company trader, Mathew Cocking, saw a Gros Ventre (Atsina) corral that had a circumference of about one hundred yards (Ewers 1949: 356). Although many of the corrals were constructed of logs, the building materials could vary. Some were built with lighter materials, and among the Cheyennes there was evidence of corrals being constructed out of brush. Apparently buffalo would not break out of a structure if they were unable to see through the walls; instead they would run around the circumference of the corral, making it easy for hunters to kill them (Grinnell 1962: 231).

In areas that buffalo were known to frequent and where the terrain was favorable, relatively permanent buffalo pounds were built and used year after year. Archaeological evidence indicates that Northern Plains hunters drove buffalo over cliffs, into corrals, and into cul-de-sacs for a very long time period (Frison 1978: 58). Thus the knowledge and skills associated with this type of hunting were deeply shared, very old traditions that informed the societies encountered by Europeans. These traditions had been learned from predecessors and transmitted from generation to generation.

The knowledge and skills surrounding butchering animals and processing their flesh for food and their hides for other uses also had deep cultural roots (see Frison 1978: 301–16). Once killed, buffalo had to be butchered, the flesh eaten on the spot or preserved for future use, the hide removed, and the other useful parts of the animal taken. According to George Bird Grinnell, among the Blackfeet

> Almost every part of the beast was utilized. The skin, dressed with the hair on, protected them from the winter's cold; freed from the hair, it was used for a summer sheet or blanket, for moccasins, leggings, shirts, and women's

dresses. The tanned cowskins made their lodges the warmest and most portable shelters ever devised. From the rawhide . . . were made parfleches, or trunks, in which to pack small articles. The tough, thick hide of the bull's neck . . . made a shield for war which would stop an arrow, and turn a lance thrust or the ball from an old-fashioned smooth-bore gun. The green hide served as a kettle, in which to boil meat. (Grinnell 1962: 127)

Smaller household articles such as quivers, gun cases, and braided rawhide ropes were also made from the skin of the buffalo, and from their hooves the Blackfeet extracted a glue to fasten feathers to their arrow shafts.

Tanning was done by rubbing a mixture of brains and liver on the hide after the flesh had been removed with a bone scraper; if the hair was to be removed, it would also have been scraped off before tanning began. Scraping off the flesh or hair was done by women, who staked out the hide on the ground. After the flesh and perhaps the hair were removed, the hides were rubbed with a brain and liver mixture and then soaked in warm water. They were then wrung out and scraped again until the desired texture was achieved. Sometimes the hides were drawn on a leather thong that was tied between two posts or trees, a process that aided in the hides' softening.

Hunting and butchering among the Blackfeet were done predominately by men, although women assisted in this process as well. Women had responsibility for dressing and tanning the hides, making clothing, utensils, and the tipi covers, as well as cooking and food preparation. Men constructed their weapons (before the gun), as well as some of their ritual objects. Women owned the food after it had been brought to the lodge, the lodge itself, and the property that was carried in the hide bags they had made (Wissler 1911: 27–28). While this division of labor seems unequal, the heavier burdens being borne by women, women also played an essential role in ritual processes that, in some instances, made the distribution of social power more equitable. These aspects of women's roles will be taken up in the chapters that follow.

After the animal was gutted and the flesh was cut from the bones, what was not consumed immediately was dried for future use. Preparation for drying involved cutting the meat into thin strips and hanging it over a rack to dry either in the sun or over a fire. This was an important step, since during warm weather flies were drawn in great numbers to the kill sites, and the meat was in danger of becoming flyblown and subsequently filled with maggots. Hanging the meat over a fire or to dry in the sun produced a hard surface in a very short time. At this point, flies could not penetrate the film to lay their eggs, and any eggs that had been deposited in the meat could not hatch. A potentially bad situation received a simple solution both in prehistoric and in later times (Frison 1978: 302–3).[3]

The primary flesh food among the Blackfeet, as was the case with most other Northern Plains peoples, was acquired from the buffalo. Northern Plains villagers, such as the Mandans and Hidatsas, had developed very successful dual economies featuring both buffalo hunting and the cultivation of corn, beans, squash, and sunflower seeds. Animals such as deer, elk, and moose were also hunted by all Northern Plains groups, but the buffalo produced the greatest amount of meat for the least hunting effort. Like humans everywhere, the Blackfeet developed a food culture that, while it varied somewhat from that of their neighbors, was not entirely distinctive (Wissler 1910: 42). Blood's description of this food culture provides a vivid portrait of Blackfoot butchering and of their food preferences.

His memories included food production for family use as well as production of finished buffalo hides that were traded for tobacco, ammunition, guns, and other items available from the traders in Blackfoot country. His description began with late spring hunting of buffalo bulls, which by this time of the year had shed their winter coats. These hunts were conducted on horseback and involved a number of people surrounding the herd and pursuing them on the run while shooting as many as were needed. Describing the butchering, Blood said that the men started the skinning from "the back down. Then they would throw out their kidneys. And the oil and grease would gather about their navels. They would throw down the yellow back-fat and spread it out. The man would tell his wife: Take and wash the manifold. When she came back, he would say to her: That leg-bone, just break that. It would be broken for him. And the manifold and the marrow of the leg would burst by chewing. He would roll the marrow in the manifold" (Uhlenbeck 1913: 2).

Another Piegan, Weasel Tail, remembered that it was during this butchering process that hunters might eat portions of the liver, kidneys, and brisket raw, and after the hunters had taken their portion, the meat was divided among the families of the camp (Ewers 1949: 360). Feasting was a common practice, according to Blood, and invitations went out regularly after a successful hunt. The hunter's relatives, particularly his wife's parents, would receive the meat. Then some of the choicest parts might be fed to the hunter, such as "the broken boss-rib, the short rib, the gut with the blood in it, the tripe where it is good" (Uhlenbeck 1913: 2). The circulation of food to the families and the entire encampment assured that the old, the infirm, and the less fortunate would have adequate nutrition and that hunters could demonstrate their generosity, which provided them with status in the group.

Blood also described the activities of women in the late summer, when they gathered sarvis berries and choke cherries, which were eaten fresh as well as dried, pounded, and mixed with soup or used to make pemmican (Uhlenbeck 1913: 4). During the midsummer, between the middle of June and the middle of July, the camas root was gathered, roasted, and then dried. Bitterroot was also gathered and dried for later consumption (Grinnell 1962: 204). During the summer and fall the hunting of buffalo continued as the group that Blood described moved about from place to place. Their movements were not random but were coordinated with the rhythms of the buffalo, the ripening of roots and berries, and the unfolding of the seasons. Their activities were structured by the projects that had to be accomplished in order both to sustain daily life and to insure that life would flourish in the coming year.

By the late fall, lodges would have been repaired or new ones constructed, new clothing and household items would have been made, and a supply of dried meat, pemmican, and dried roots and vegetables would have been laid in. During the crisp days of late fall the people moved closer to the mountains, where they hunted deer, elk, and moose. During this time, according to Blood, the people began to enjoy what was a favorite food item among the Blackfeet—soup made from guts, tripe, fat, and dried berries. "No one," said Blood, "would turn his head away from the soup" (Uhlenbeck 1913: 7).

In the late fall, after the first snow, the people would move to lower elevations near streams and rivers, where they would spend the winter. The buffalo now possessed luxuriant winter coats, and the hunters continued to kill animals both for meat and for robes that would warm their families during the winter. If the year had been a good one, then the beginning of winter was positively anticipated, according to Blood: "Oh, happy times there would be in the beginning of the winter, from the food that they got" (Uhlenbeck 1913: 8). Blood's description recalls Marshall Sahlins's understanding of the "original affluent society" of hunters and gatherers who were normally able to satisfy all of their material needs and have time left over for ritual and leisure (1972: 1).

While there was certainly affluence in Sahlins's sense during good years, Blood's memories also reflected the influence of the fur trade. As the trade expanded, Northern Plains peoples acquired guns, ammunition, metal pots, cloth, beads, tobacco, and other items from the traders in exchange for buffalo robes and pemmican. Rather than producing to meet the people's needs, hunters and the women who processed the meat began to produce surpluses for purposes of trade. According to Blood, when the people had sufficient food for themselves they took the surpluses to the trading post: "They all went on [to the trading post] to buy powder, hard cartridges, tobacco, white blankets, black blankets; such things they would buy. One blanket costed five robes, [another] blanket costed four robes. Powder [one gallon] costed one robe. A hundred cartridges costed two robes. Flints, [and] black gun-springs costed together one robe. Only four [plugs] of tobacco were [to be bought for] one robe. . . . Such things they would buy" (Uhlenbeck 1913: 14). While these exchanges expanded the material base of Northern Plains societies, it is possible to look back and see in retrospect that the very processes that stimulated new social energies led finally to destructive consequences for these peoples.

Among the Blackfeet, the place where buffalo were killed, whether by being driven over a cliff or into a corral, was called a *piskun*. George Bird Grinnell initially translated this word as "deep-kettle," but because of the word's construction, which suggested the additional meaning of "blood," his final translation was "deep-blood-kettle" (Grinnell 1962: 228). Whether this translation was completely adequate or not does not detract from its powerful and suggestive imagery: the places where large numbers of animals were killed were bathed in blood and contained numerous fleshy bones that were eventually picked clean by smaller predators. They could also be identified at great distances by the powerful odor emitted by rotting flesh.

The description of buffalo hunting provided by Blood included details that require further analysis (Uhlenbeck 1913: 38–41). He described, for example, religious practices that were associated with hunting. After the corral was built or one that was previously in use had been repaired, Blood said, the chief called the people together and announced the hunt. During the construction or repair of the corral, he, along with medicine persons, had been praying for the success of the hunt (cf. Grinnell 1962: 229; Wissler 1910: 33–52). Informed by the prayers of the medicine persons, the chief would appoint a leader of the hunt.

On the day of the hunt, the leader who was to call the animals put on a buffalo headdress and covered his body with a buffalo robe. He went out to the herd, making body movements that attracted the animals' attention. Once he got their attention and they began to follow him, the hunt leader moved faster and faster, leading the animals into the drive lane. Behind the piles of stone forming the drive lines people were concealed. "When the buffalo ran between those piles of stones," Blood said, "then the buffalo-leader ran to the side. . . . Then they scared the buffalo with the leg-parts of their robes . . . and [the buffalo] jumped over [the cliff]" (Uhlenbeck 1913: 39). Each hunter had marked his arrows so that he could tell which kill he had made, and when the corral was filled with animals, the slaughter began. In this description, however, the killing was limited by the people's needs as they understood them. "All the people climbed up to the corral. From there they shot down. When the buffalo were running around, they would not kill them all. They only killed the bulls that they needed. And to the others they opened the corral. And they ran out" (Uhlenbeck 1913: 40).

The pattern of reliance upon medicine persons and ritual processes when engaged in communal hunting was widespread on the Northern Plains. In addition to the Blackfeet, there are typical examples among the Crees (Mandelbaum 1940: 190–91) and the Lakotas (Walker 1982a: 74–94), as well as the village dwelling Mandans and Hidatsas (Bowers 1965: 54). Clearly the role of medicine persons was viewed by these people as essential to the hunting process; without the prayers, use of sacred objects, and the enactment of rituals, they believed that the hunt would be in jeopardy. Chapter 5 discusses these buffalo-calling rituals in greater detail, but at this point it is important to envision something of their historical importance.

Northern Plains archaeological evidence points to the ancient role played by religious specialists, especially in the communal hunt. A fascinating example is provided by a late second-century buffalo corral known as the Ruby site located in the southeastern part of the Powder River Basin in Wyoming (Frison 1978: 213–21). The bone beds at this site indicate that it was used for many years. The construction of the corral also indicates that these early hunters were quite sophisticated, successful hunters. The work that was required to construct a corral of some forty feet in diameter, using wooden and bone digging sticks, was enormous. The effort, practical knowledge, and skills required to build the corral were also deeply intertwined with knowledge about how to relate to powers that transcended the hunter's efforts. These powers were invoked through the ritual work that was done by religious specialists at the hunting site.

For example, at the Ruby site there was, in addition to the corral, another structure that bore strong evidence of religious activities. Buffalo vertebrae buried in holes around this structure may have originally been oriented to the cardinal directions, and eight male buffalo skulls were placed at the south end of the structure (Frison 1978: 220). Rituals featuring buffalo neck bones as well as buffalo skulls were widespread among the people who occupied the Northern Plains at the time of European contact. Because of the long time intervals, it is clearly impossible to claim a continuity of cultural *identity* between the hunters who used the Ruby site in the second century and the hunters who built buffalo corrals and employed hunting rituals during the eighteenth and nineteenth centuries. But there was evidence of similar cultural *practices*, including religious rituals, between these two vastly separated time periods. Even though evidence of ritual language that may have been used in these earlier times is impossible to recover, a Cree welcome to the buffalo as they entered the corral may be illustrative of earlier attitudes: "My Grandfather, we are glad to see you, and happy that you are not come in a shameful manner, for you have brought plenty of your young men with you.

Be not angry with us; we are obliged to destroy you to make ourselves live"
(Milloy 1988: 103).

While it is impossible to reconstruct the religious dimensions of the lives
of early hunters, it is possible to recover some of the sensibilities of the hunters who were encountered by Europeans on the Northern Plains. These hunters
participated in highly developed, though not unchanging, symbolic universes.
The ritual processes that surrounded hunting were complex and had a long
history. This history was as much a history of change as it was of continuity,
since many of the peoples that Europeans encountered were migrants to the
Northern Plains. An exploration of these symbolic universes and the ritual
processes generated in them allows us to begin to reconstruct some understanding of their richly imagined views of animals. The next chapter begins
that process by examining the primordial relations with animals that were
portrayed in Northern Plains origin traditions.

2

in the

beginning
there

were

animals

In the last chapter we saw how Northern Plains peoples hunted and killed animals, processed their flesh, and created a rich food culture based primarily upon the buffalo. What was not so clearly visible was how these activities were interpenetrated by meanings mediated by the symbolic forms embodied in their oral traditions and enacted in their ritual processes. Understanding the deeper significance of hunting, killing, and consuming animals as food requires that we bring more clearly into view broader horizons of meaning embodied in the complex networks of cultural symbols that characterized Northern Plains oral traditions. This chapter begins this task by looking at origin traditions that portrayed primordial relations between humans and animals. These traditions were sedimented in cultural symbols that shaped the way perception and concrete experience were organized and gave rise to a shared understanding of the world. A study of origin traditions lays the groundwork for interpreting the animal rituals that are the subject of the chapters to follow.

It is well known among students of these traditions that there was no single, authoritative, standard, or "canonical" version. Even though this is acknowledged, there is evidence to show that there was usually a basic meaning complex that characterized several versions of a particular narrative. But there is also evidence that indicates that there were fundamental additions to as well as creative transformations of these traditions. Creative transformations in meaning were often part of a broader process of reinterpretation, and such processes of reinterpretation sometimes reflected creative attempts to come to terms with fundamental social changes such as those introduced by epidemic diseases and migrations.[1]

Another feature that is important for understanding these traditions has to do with the differences—as well as blurred boundaries—between the primary characters that were central to these narratives. For example, in the origin traditions there were differences between creator figures, tricksters, and culture heroes, and there were instances when boundaries between these figures became blurred. In some traditions, creator figures were primarily responsible for the origins of the earth, human beings, animals, the structure of gender relations, and death. Trickster figures, as well as creator figures who embodied these features, sometimes shared in the creation of the human beings, the arrangement of human destiny, and the shape of the geography that constituted a particular people's homeland. Tricksters were typically possessed by rampant hungers, including enormous sexual appetites, and they often did foolish and destructive things either to themselves or to the animals. Culture heroes brought the people particular gifts such as hunting rituals and symbolic objects such as bundles or pipes that were essential to the people's life. But since origin narratives on the Northern Plains sometimes included creator figures who had trickster characteristics as well as culture hero features, any classification of these narratives must retain fluid boundaries in order to represent what actually seems to be going on in the narratives.[2]

A somewhat deeper problem has to do with the fundamental transformations in meaning that occurred when traditions that were essentially oral performances, in which meaning was dependent upon the narrator's presentational style, were reduced to texts (Walker 1983: 29; cf. Hymes 1981; Kroeber

1981). It is often impossible to know either what the oral contexts of presentation were or the identity of the narrator or narrators. Some of the English texts, such as George Dorsey's presentation of a version of an Arapaho creation tradition, bore clear traces of oral performance, as did some of the Crow texts published by Robert Lowie. But it is impossible to recover the dramatic pauses, facial expressions, and tone of voice of the narrator, all of which would be essential to interpreting the fuller meaning of the tradition. Despite these problems, it is possible to find in these narratives-become-texts core images and meanings that were widely shared and persisted through time.

An examination of indigenous categories that functioned to distinguish between various types of narratives provides us with some additional understanding of how Northern Plains peoples may have viewed their traditions of origin.[3] While Clark Wissler did not give a precise characterization of indigenous categories, he did claim that, among the Blackfeet, "mythical characters [such as those in the origin accounts] are generally accorded the same reality as pertains to a deceased friend" (Wissler and Duvall 1908: 17). At the beginning of the twentieth century, then, the more important characters in Blackfoot traditions were viewed as having played essential roles in the Blackfoot past. Given this interpretation, the origin traditions of the Blackfeet were probably classified as having to do with real characters and events that occurred when the world was coming into being. As we will learn presently, these characters continue to play a role in contemporary Blackfoot life.

Another Blackfoot classification distinguished origin traditions from those that apparently represented the remembered past of the people. These narratives, which often had to do with a distant past, began with linguistic markers that identified them as stories believed to be about the experiences of predecessors. For example, when traditions began with references to the akai-Pekaniua (the ancient Piegans) or to the akaitapiua (the ancient people), then these narratives were probably accepted as true remembrances of the group's past.[4]

In a somewhat similar manner, the Crows distinguished between narratives that represented what was believed to be the lived past of predecessors and those that represented a more distant past (Lowie 1918: 13). These latter traditions were, in my view, considered to be true, but they focused upon events and the activities of nonhuman persons who existed before the appearance of the present world. The Crow creation accounts belonged to this category.

The Pawnees made a distinction between traditions that represented things that actually happened, either in the experience of the people or in long past times when the world was coming into being, and traditions that were not true in this sense but were constructed by elders usually for the purpose of providing examples of good moral life as well as examples of opposite—usually Trickster—forms of behavior (Dorsey 1906: 10). In many Northern Plains cultures, Trickster behavior provided a negative moral example since this character usually violated the established values of the group (Harrod 1987: 63–65).

Lakota traditions were divided into two main groups, each of which contained two subdivisions. The linguistic markers that distinguished these forms of tradition appeared in the oral performances and were clearly understood by the hearers (Deloria 1932: ix–x; Walker 1983: 25). For example, in the early part of the twentieth century, Lakotas spoke of a group of narratives that contained elements of the fantastic and incredible. This body of traditions was subdivided into two parts, the first of which may represent a very old layer that might have been viewed differently in an earlier time. This group included traditions featuring characters that were clearly more than human but that were sometimes represented as having relations with past humans. These stories were deeply shared and were a "part of the common literary stock of the people. Constant allusion is made to them; similes are drawn from them which every intelligent adult is sure to understand" (Deloria 1932: ix). Clearly these traditions were deeply embedded in shared symbolic structures and represented the long-ago past before the present world was fully formed. I think it is reasonable to assume that because these traditions were so pervasive, they may have been viewed by Lakota predecessors as describing real events and transcendent persons. The second subdivision contained traditions that featured elements of the fantastic, but the godlike beings of the first category have disappeared. Although set in the distant past, the people believed that happenings like those described in the narratives might actually have taken place.

The second main category included traditions describing events that were believed to be within the historical memory of the group. The first subdivision contained narratives that pertained to experiences that were relevant to the Lakota people as a whole (e.g., Wounded Knee), while the second subdivision embodied more local traditions that were peculiar to the experience of a particular group. These traditions constituted the shared memory of the group as well as the more specific memories of particular subgroups.

The origin narratives of Northern Plains peoples usually took the form of a complex representation of actions of animal figures, creator/trickster figures (often in animal form), and other "powers," such as Wind, Sun, Moon, and Stars. The world as it was known in present experience was brought into being by the actions of these beings. Northern Plains origin traditions also exhibited a pattern that was widely shared among peoples who were otherwise linguistically and culturally differentiated. This pattern has been identified by folklorists as the "earth diver" motif. Even though there were internal variations, the narratives exhibited essentially the same structure: there were primal waters, one or more creator figures, animals or birds who retrieved earth from below the surface of the waters, and the use of this material by the creator figure(s) to form the earth as it was then known and experienced.[5] While this narrative structure was very widespread among Northern Plains peoples, the creator figures as well as some of the other characters in the narratives possessed different identities and were culturally related to the people who shared the tradition. In this way the narratives functioned to form the social identity of particular peoples, and as long as the traditions were deeply sedimented in experience, their sense of shared identity was maintained.

Origin traditions among the Blackfeet, who were Algonquian-speaking buffalo hunters, formed a similar deep layer of meaning and contributed to a world picture that was shared at a very general level. It is important to understand that these shared meanings probably arose as a consequence of gradual cultural accretion. Nineteenth- and early twentieth-century origin traditions may have been quite different from the traditions that constituted the Blackfoot understanding before their migration to the Northern Plains from the eastern woodlands. Even so, elements that were so characteristic in the early twentieth century represented meanings that had persisted over a relatively long time period and formed a core of symbolic meanings that was transmitted from generation to generation. The first of these elements was the figure of Napi, or Old Man, who was the generative source of Blackfoot life and the universe. The second element was primal waters, below which earth waited to be brought to the surface to become material for Napi's world-creating activity. The third element was a company of animals and birds that was present with Napi at the "beginning" and that assisted the creator in his generative acts.

The details often varied, but the notion of primal waters persisted. In one version, Napi was portrayed as surrounded by waters that took the form of a raging flood; he sought to escape from the rising waters by running from one place to another until finally he reached a high mountain (Wissler 1946: 7). In another version, Old Man was sitting on the highest mountain (Wissler and Duvall 1908: 19), and in a third version he was perched on a log floating on the surface of the water (McLean 1892: 165).

In all of these traditions, Napi was surrounded by preexisting animals. In one version he was represented as being in the company of all of the animals (Wissler and Duvall 1908: 19). But in this and other traditions, Napi was assisted in his world-building activities by four creatures whose life was fundamentally characterized by an existence on or under the water. At the deeper symbolic level, these traditions represented Napi as drawing upon the power of these water creatures, indeed as *needing* their assistance in the formation of the world. The fundamental dependence upon animal life and animal power that characterized the Blackfoot experience found its charter in Napi's dependence on these animal persons, and the creator's need for animal assistance suggested a being who was far from perfect and all-powerful.

The animal assistants varied among versions—beaver, otter, duck, and muskrat (Wissler 1946: 7; Wissler and Duvall 1908: 19); fish, frog, lizard, and turtle (McLean 1892: 165)—but each of them was viewed as possessing water power, which the creator needed to accomplish his task. The Blackfeet knew that their world and its landforms arose through the transformative activity of Napi, although the effort required to acquire the appropriate materials (earth from beneath the waters) was provided through the agency of the animals. One by one these animals dove below the surface, but the first three attempts ended in failure, and the animals sacrificed their lives. The fourth diving animal—in one version a duck, in another a muskrat, and in another a turtle—was successful. The earth that was retrieved from beneath the waters was taken by Napi, who "put it in his hand, feigned putting it on the water three times, and at last dropped it. Then the above-people sent rain, and everything grew on the earth" (Wissler and Duvall 1908: 19).

The core features of this narrative are still known among the Blackfeet who live on reservations in northwestern Montana and in Alberta, Canada. Traditional people on these reservations still interpret their experience in the light of contemporary versions of the Napi narrative. However, contemporary Napi traditions that are often most visible have to do with this being's exploits as a trickster figure. In this form, Napi's foolishness, hunger, and sexual appetites are the most prominent features of the narratives. When people on the Blackfeet Reservation in Montana comment on the sexual behavior of another, they still might say, "He is just acting like Napi."[6] It is symbolically appropriate that a local bar that existed for many years in Browning, Montana, was named after this colorful figure.

In the early part of the century, when Clark Wissler and D. C. Duvall were collecting traditions among the Blackfeet, the people also viewed Napi as a trickster figure and distinguished him from Natos, the Sun Man (1908: 11). Certainly Sun, Moon, and Morning Star occupied important roles in Blackfoot traditions, but it may be that the Napi earth diver traditions came from an older layer of cultural experience than those that portrayed the Sun Man (Wissler and Duvall 1908: 12).

A recent version of the origin tradition, rendered by Percy Bullchild, brings these two figures together. Bullchild's narrative had as its central character a solar figure, Creator Sun (1985: 5–8). It was this being who created the world, animals, and human beings; then, taking a part of his own spirit, he created a companion for the human beings whose name was Napi, or Old Man (Bullchild 1985: 86). This tradition is interesting not only because it combines elements of older versions but also because it creatively reinterprets these traditions in the light of more recent Blackfoot history and embodies motifs that were derived from their experience with missionaries and Christianity. For example, Creator Sun made the first human, a man, out of mud and breathed life into his nostrils. Then Mudman was put to sleep by the creator, and from his rib a woman was made. Mudman and Ribwoman were the first humans, but their beginnings clearly reflect the effects of motifs from the Hebrew creation tradition, which was mediated to the Blackfeet by missionary versions of Christianity (see Bullchild 1985: 38–52).

In this tradition, Sun creates flesh food for the people, who had up to this point been living on roots, berries, and various plant foods. In the same manner as the creation of humans, Sun shaped a four-legged male animal out of mud and blew life into his nostrils; then he took a rib from this creature and made a female animal, blowing life into her nostrils as well. This animal was named by the creator Eye-i-in-nawhw, which was translated "shall be peeled," referring to the skinning of the buffalo in order to expose its flesh for food (Bullchild 1985: 54–55). When compared with the earlier traditions, it is clear that this tradition preserved some of the central elements of the older materials, creatively reinterpreting them in the light of present Blackfoot experience.

The larger Blackfoot tradition contained many of the elements that Bullchild worked into his version, including the figure of Napi. What he does not include are the older images of primal waters and diving animals; instead, the world is made out of "space dust," which Creator Sun spit upon and then shaped into a round ball that in the future would become the earth (Bullchild 1985: 5–6). This is a creative rendering that takes into account images that contemporary Blackfeet would have encountered through television and their experiences in the public schools. It is in effect a modern Blackfoot portrait of the universe that probably includes associations with the image of the earth as it can now be seen from space, but at the same time, this is a thoroughly Blackfoot understanding.

The earlier creation narratives formed a complex symbolic network that constituted the more concrete Blackfoot experiences of both the human and the nonhuman worlds. Because they were so deeply known, these narratives functioned as frames for a distinctive Blackfoot experience of the world. This world picture was transmitted through socialization processes to Blackfeet children, and it has persisted through generational time. The possibility that a Bullchild version could have arisen demonstrates both this persistence and the capacities to creatively rework the tradition. While Napi's transformative activities were central to earlier forms of these narratives, the beings who acquired the material to be shaped into a world were the birds and animals who preexisted with the creator. For Blackfeet who hunted buffalo on the Northern Plains, this primordial relationship with animals was constitutive of their experience of the world.

The people who became the Crows were Siouan-speaking kinfolk of the Hidatsas and were once village dwellers who lived in an area where the Knife River empties into the Missouri River. Groups of these people separated from their village background and migrated west to become mobile, tipi-dwelling buffalo hunters. Their creation narratives were the symbolic source of a distinctive Crow world experience, yet with interesting similarities with Blackfoot traditions. For example, the traditions of both groups featured primal waters, diving animals or birds, and preexisting nonhuman beings; in the case of the Crows, however, the preexisting beings were both plants and animals.

These themes appeared in great detail in a version narrated by Medicine-Crow (Lowie 1918: 14–15). In this account, the creator figure was Sun, who appeared in the form of an ancient animal, Old-Man-Coyote. In another version of this tradition, narrated by Yellow-Bear, Old-Man-Coyote was not identified as Sun but rather appeared in primordial animal form (Lowie 1935: 122). And in still another version, the Crow creation narrative portrayed the origin of the earth arising initially through the activity of four water birds; only later was Old-Man-Coyote consulted (Lowie 1918: 17–19).

In Medicine Crow's narrative, where Old-Man-Coyote was identified with Sun, the creator figure's language employed familiar kinship terminology: the creator and the animals were portrayed as members of the same family, the same fundamental order of being (Lowie 1918: 14–15). Indicating to the ducks that he had prior knowledge concerning the presence of the earth below the primal waters, Old-Man-Coyote asked the largest duck, a red-headed mallard, to dive. His attempt, as well as those of two other ducks, failed. The fourth attempt was made by the smallest duck, the hell-diver, who said to the creator, "My brother, you should have asked me before the others, then you would have had land long ago. These [the larger ducks] are my superiors, yet they are helpless" (Lowie 1918: 14). Again, this narrative employed themes widespread among the Northern Plains peoples: important things were often done by the least likely beings, such as the weak, the poor, or the anonymous—in short, the marginalized in society. Furthermore, important activities often took the form of a "test" and were accomplished on the "fourth" trial (see Lowie 1908).

After mud was brought from the depths by the smallest duck, Sun took this material and, beginning in the east, spread the earth all along his westward path until the circle was completed and the circumference of the world was formed. It is evident that the symbolic forms of this narrative portrayed the formation of the world before the Crows existed as a people, but it was to be a world that they, along with other humans, would occupy. It is not clear in this narrative whether the water birds who dove for the earth preexisted with the creator or whether he was responsible for their origin. What was clear is that, as the tradition unfolds, it blooms with images of powerful beings who seem to have their own powers of generation. One of these beings, a wolf, was heard by the creator howling in the east, while another, a coyote, was heard yipping in the west. Of the coyote, Sun said, "That coyote has attained life by his own powers, he is great" (Lowie 1918: 15).

In addition to these autochthonous animal persons, Sun and his duck companions encountered a medicine stone who had the capacity to reproduce himself. This stone was judged to be the "oldest" part of the earth and to possess great power, symbolized by his capacity for self-generation. In addition to this deep earth person, they encountered a sky person in the form of a Star Man. As they approached, the Star Person transformed himself into a tobacco plant; at this time there were no other plants in existence. Clearly this plant possessed powers that were separate from and as impressive as those of the creator and his duck companions.

A review of the images packed into this tradition reveals that there were many powerful persons besides Sun who appeared in the figure of Old-Man-Coyote. All of these beings contributed in their own way to the formation of the world; indeed, some of them were self-generating, a part of reality before the world came into being. Likewise, the primal sea contained mysterious depths below which were powerful substances such as earth, and there were water birds that had the power to negotiate these depths in a way that the creator could not. In addition to these underneath places, there were powerful sky figures, such as the Star Man, who made essential contributions to the formation of the "middle reality" of the earth.

In another Crow account, the earth arose as a consequence of the formative activity of two beings, Old-Man-Coyote and his younger brother, who was called Cirape, a little coyote (Lowie 1918: 17–19; 1935: 122–31). Together they fashioned the earth, created its landforms, and populated it with plants, animals, and human beings (Crows). The process of creating life forms involved a sense of radical contingency, experimentation, and trial and error on the part of the creator figures—it could well have been otherwise! Likewise, the relations between the animals and their creator were not always harmonious.

For example, after Old-Man-Coyote had created the bear, this animal denied his origins, claiming that he had created himself. In fact, this narrative portrayed Bear as an arrogant bully who mistreated the other animals and who tried to bully Old-Man-Coyote as well (Lowie 1935: 127). Bear challenged Old-Man-Coyote to create other life forms; only then would he believe the claims about his origin. In response to this challenge, Old-Man-Coyote created a bird out of various materials: a piece of buffalo muscle, coyote and bear claws, a little hairy worm, and box elder leaves to form the bird's tail. Old-Man-Coyote then painted the bird a grayish color, but, upon finishing, he decided that the color was not right, and he repainted the bird with the colors it presently has; thus was the origin of the prairie chicken (Lowie 1935: 125). After this demonstration Bear was convinced and grudgingly acknowledged that Old-Man-Coyote's words about his origins were true.

After the human beings were created, Old-Man-Coyote and Cirape decreed that the people should eat plants as well as animals, that they should build dwellings in which to live, and that they should have fire with which to cook their food. But because the animals were so powerful, intelligent, and quick compared to the humans, some advantage had to be given to the humans if they were to hunt the animals for food. Old-Man-Coyote and Cirape decided that the human beings would possess arms with which to hunt the animals, but the animals would not possess weapons (Lowie 1935: 127–28).

These traditions exhibited a variety of often contradictory relations, tensions, and unresolved aspects. To add to this creative mix, there was another Crow tradition that had the standard features of primal waters and four ducks (Lowie 1918: 17–19), but in this version the ducks decided on their own to dive below the water in order to bring up soil. Clearly these duck beings possessed great power and agency; they were masters of the underwater world and had the autonomous capacity to acquire the materials for making a world. In addition, they actually possessed the power to give initial form to the world. After one duck was successful in bringing up earth, they proceeded with their constructive activity. The world they created was a flat place, and there were no people yet on the earth.

At this point the ducks, who were dissatisfied with their work, decided to consult with Old-Man-Coyote and to ask for his advice in this matter. In response to their request, Old-Man-Coyote gave further shape to the land, making mountains, valleys, trees, and other vegetation. Even though Old-Man-Coyote was represented as having greater creative power compared to the ducks, they were clearly possessed of significant power themselves. Old-Man-Coyote had already made people (when this took place the tradition does not say), but they remained unfinished and were encased in the hollows of the trees. He took an ax, chopped down a tree, and a human being came forth. These beings had no eyes, so the creator tore open eye slits in the first human and instructed this person to do the same for the human beings who were to follow.

After the emergence of the humans, Old-Man-Coyote instructed them in all the arts of living, created animals and plants to be their food, and taught the people how to make weapons. He also taught them how to hunt animals by driving them down a sloping ridge into a corral. At this time the tradition represented the buffalo as living like coyotes in dens in the ground. For some reason unspecified in the narrative, these animals had disappeared and were not available to the human beings for food. After a long search, Cirape was successful in discovering the buffalo den and bringing the buffalo to the surface of the earth. The tradition ended with the image of two human hunters following the tracks of the newly emerged buffalo.

The Algonquian-speaking Arapahos shared creation narratives that focused on the image of a living being floating on the surface of primal waters (Dorsey and Kroeber 1903: 1–6). The formula that introduced one of these narratives would be deeply familiar to Northern Plains peoples: the person floating on the water was fasting and crying, seeking power to accomplish something good. The language of the account indicated that the creator figure was appealing to a higher power, a "Grandfather," for assistance. Seeing that the person was sincere in his intent, the Grandfather granted him power to call on all of the water birds for assistance.

The creator being, who was sitting on a tripod and was, in actuality, a flat-pipe-person, was identified as the father of the Indians. In Arapaho experience, this flat-pipe-person played an essential role in establishing their identity as a people. For them, the flat pipe was central to many of their ritual processes and was normally kept in a bundle that was mounted on top of a tripod. Thus the images that formed this version of the creation narrative would have been quite familiar to Arapaho persons hearing the story.

The Arapaho accounts were similar to those of other Northern Plains peoples in that water birds were enlisted to dive below the surface to bring up earth. In the case of these traditions, however, the turtle was the only underwater creature with sufficient power to reach the bottom and bring up enough earth to create the world. Duck had succeeded in bringing up a small bit of earth in his claws, but it was not enough for the job. When Turtle finally emerged from beneath the waters, the creator took the mud from his four feet and spread it out to dry; when it was dry, he blew the soil toward each of the four directions and then, swinging his arm in a circular motion, he cast forth the remaining earth, and the world arose.[7]

There was a longer, much more detailed version told in connection with the Sun Dance (Dorsey 1903: 191–228). This narrative reproduced some of the richness of the oral performance and included elements not found in more abbreviated accounts. In addition to the flat-pipe-person, the tradition introduced a trickster figure who possessed significant power and who made additions to the creation; he also engaged in foolish and destructive activities. In this tradition the central creator figure also had the ability to appear in more than one form.

This tradition opened, as did some of the others, with a fasting, praying figure who was walking about on the waters carrying with him an object of great significance and value—a flat pipe. After considering his options, this person decided to create an earth in order to have a place for the flat pipe to be kept and honored. But he could not do his work alone. Calling in a loud but respectful voice to each of the four directions, the creator figure summoned all of the animals and birds to come and help search for earth below the waters. After all of these preexisting animal and bird persons arrived, they talked excitedly about the task that lay before them.

The creator asked if any of the animals had heard of earth in the underwater country, implying that he had no knowledge himself concerning such material. Later on in the narrative it became clear that the creator knew of the existence of earth deep below the surface but that he had consciously withheld this information in order to structure the occasion in the form of a test for the animals. Finally, after much discussion, Turtle was the only creature who claimed to have certain knowledge of what lay beneath the surface of the water.

Five unsuccessful attempts were made by water birds and water animals; and on a sixth attempt all of the animals and birds who had gathered from the four directions made a dive together, but all came to the surface without having found earth. The language of the narrative was such that the reader (and hearer) would understand that the creator figure had known all along that they would be unsuccessful and that only Turtle had both knowledge about the underwater world and the endurance to make a successful dive. At this point it was agreed that Turtle and the creator figure would make the seventh attempt. The figure who appeared at the beginning of the narrative in the form of a man took the flat pipe and "embraced himself with it, first to the left shoulder, then to the right shoulder, then back to the left, then to the right, and lastly to his breast. At this fifth time, the Flat-Pipe became his body . . . it adhered to him in the center, having turned into a red-head duck" (Dorsey 1903: 197).

The man-flat-pipe-duck dove below the surface and, along with Turtle, swam down into the dark waters. All of the animals waited anxiously for seven days for their return; finally, as the sun was about to set on the last day, they saw bubbles rising to the surface of the water. First to come up was the red-head duck, who swam to his original place. Suddenly the man holding the flat pipe appeared again at his original place on the waters. The narrative then represented the man receiving earth from both Turtle and Duck. He spread it out on the flat pipe to dry, after which he cast it toward the four cardinal directions. Because of the importance of Turtle in the creation of the world, the creator decreed that from that time forward his body would be a symbol for the earth. It is also significant that in this version of the tradition, the buffalo (White-Buffalo) gave himself to the people for food and for clothing.

The Atsinas, or Gros Ventres of Montana (not to be confused with the Hidatsas, who were also referred to as Gros Ventres), were a small group of Algonquian-speaking people who were often allied with the Blackfeet. One version of their origin tradition had interesting similarities with Arapaho narratives since the creator figure was a man who was the keeper of a Flat Pipe (Cooper 1957: 435–37). In this narrative, which may reflect Christian missionary influence, the keeper of the Flat Pipe had survived a great flood. He built a raft and was floating on it with his Flat Pipe when he saw in the distance a great mountain thrusting up out of the water; there were birds and a few animals on the mountain who had also survived the flood.

While we might expect the keeper of the Flat Pipe to create the earth out of material provided by the mountain, the narrative instead moved through a typical earth diver sequence. While singing a powerful song, the pipe keeper cast earth that had been retrieved by the water animals and birds toward each of the four directions. After he had created earth, the keeper took a bit of mud and created a man shape; after breathing on it, a human being appeared. Out of the rib of the man this being created a woman (recall this motif in the Blackfoot version by Percy Bullchild), and the world was populated as a consequence of the fruitful relationship between these two humans.

The Assiniboines, who were a Siouan-speaking group, shared an origin story that, while appearing in the form of an earth diver account, had its own cultural specificity. The creator figure in this account exhibited trickster features and was known among the people as Iktomi (Lowie 1909: 100–105). The narrative opened with Iktomi traveling about on the surface of the water in a boat covered with moose skin. Unlike the Blackfoot or the Crow account, this version of the narrative did not represent Iktomi as having any special intentionality or purpose; he did not seem to be thinking about or intending to create a world. Rather, the creation of the earth was occasioned by a chance meeting on the surface of the waters between Iktomi and a muskrat. Muskrat had a bit of mud in his paws, which initially he did not wish to show to Iktomi. After an offer to enter the boat if he revealed what he had in his paws, the muskrat showed the mud to Iktomi, who took it, blew upon it, and formed the earth. Another recorded version of this narrative does include the image of a more intentional creation: Iktomi sent animals diving for earth, but no animal was able to succeed. Finally, Muskrat dove below the surface, and, even though he was dead when he resurfaced, he had a bit of mud in his paw out of which the creator-trickster formed the earth (Lowie 1909: 101).

Trickster features also appeared in other Assiniboine traditions. In one narrative Iktomi wore a wolf-skin robe, which perhaps may be interpreted as a sign of his shape-shifting character. After the world was created, he asserted that there would be winter for as many months as there were hairs on the wolf skin. Frog demurred: "If the winter lasts as long as that, no creature will be able to live. Seven months of winter will be enough" (Lowie 1909: 101). Frog kept repeating his objection until finally Iktomi, in a rage, killed him. Even in death, Frog stretched out seven of his toes, and after seeing them, Iktomi relented.

In a longer narrative (Lowie 1909: 101–5) the trickster elements of Iktomi's personality were also evident as, along with a number of animal helpers, he orchestrated the theft of summer from a man far to the east who kept this season in a bag. In this version Frog was present with his pipe, and when he suggested that there be only six months of winter, Iktomi struck him on the head with a club, knocking him to the ground and stunning him. After Frog stretched out his hands (showing six fingers), Iktomi took pity on him and agreed to the division of the seasons, putting Frog in charge of the winter season. Unlike some of the previous narratives, this Assiniboine tradition contained elements of tension and deceit that characterized the relations between Iktomi and the animals. These qualities were probably viewed as a natural consequence of Iktomi's trickster nature.

One version of a Cheyenne origin tradition included not only the typical diving birds and the creation of the earth but also an image of seasonal powers who were under the control of two persons, a woman and a man, who had been created after the formation of the world and placed in the north and south, respectively (Grinnell 1971: 242–44). The gray-haired woman in the north was in control of Winter Man, the power who brought snow and cold as well as the sickness and death associated with winter; though her hair was gray, she did not grow older. The man in the south was in control of Thunder, the power associated with spring and summer rains and the growth of animals and plants. Thunder also had knowledge of fire. With the assistance of the buffalo, Thunder made fire and transmitted this knowledge to human beings (who were created sometime after the first two persons) through one of the Cheyenne culture heroes, Sweet Medicine.

The Arikaras, who were Caddoan-speaking people, were once a division of the Skidi Pawnees. They shared an origin tradition that included in one of its versions two figures known as Lucky Man and Wolf (Dorsey 1904a: 11). These two beings came to the shore of a huge lake, Lucky Man from the north and Wolf from the southwest. They met on the shore of the lake and were immediately engaged in a contest: Wolf challenged Lucky Man, claiming that he could better endure the chilling rain that was falling. Wolf had his own skin for protection, and Lucky Man tried to protect himself by tying some feathers on a stick. Wolf was defeated in this contest, but both of these powerful beings agreed to create the earth together. Wolf took earth that had been brought from the bottom of the lake by a duck and cast it to the north, creating grasslands upon which buffalo grazed. Lucky Man took his turn, casting toward the south the earth that a second duck had brought to the surface, creating hills and mountains in that direction. After the land to the north and south had been created, a great river began to flow between them: "The first thing they [Lucky Man and Wolf] knew, the stream of the Missouri began to flow along the dividing line of the two countries they had created" (Dorsey 1904a: 11).

According to one Arikara tradition, humans arose from the spider people. This tradition included not only Spider-Man and his wife but also Wolf and his companion (Lucky Man?). The spider people were represented as dirty and repulsive. For example, "The Spider-Man was dirty, his eyes were red, he had no hair on his head, and he was very dirty all over, and he emitted a bad odor. His wife also was very dirty; her hair was thin and very coarse" (Dorsey 1904a: 12).

At this point the transcription lapsed into Latin (typical of Dorsey and other ethnographers of his period when sexual matters were discussed). Wolf asked the spider people how they had sexual intercourse. Rather than describe the act, they provided a demonstration. In this way Wolf discovered that they had many genitalia that smelled very bad. Repelled by the sight and smell of the spider people, Wolf suggested that he and his friend (Lucky Man?) could help them to look better and teach them to have sexual intercourse in a more appropriate manner. "So the Wolf and his friend went and got some wild sage and fixed up some medicine. They dipped the wild sage into the water and rubbed it all over the two Spider people. As they rubbed the wild sage over them they became very different, they looked better, and did not smell bad" (Dorsey 1904a: 12). Then Wolf taught the spider people how to have sexual intercourse and how to conceive children. As a consequence of these acts, the human beings were born. Presumably no human beings would have appeared had Wolf and his friend not intervened, transforming the spider beings into persons who could give rise to the humans.

The significance of the Missouri River as a source of many fundamental cultural symbols was important not only for the Arikaras but also for village groups to the north, the Siouan-speaking Mandans and Hidatsas. They shared a tradition that emphasized in a more specific manner than some of the other Northern Plains traditions the creation of particular landforms that became the homeland of the people.

The Mandan-Hidatsa narrative shared with some other Northern Plains traditions two beings who were involved in the creation of the earth: Lone Man and Coyote, also known as First Man (compare the tradition of the Crows). What is interesting about this tradition are the deep symbolic meanings surrounding both plants and animals that it evoked. For example, Lone Man was typified as walking on the surface of primal water, and as he walked he engaged in deep thought concerning his own origins. Looking back from whence he came, Lone Man could see his tracks on the surface of the water.

Following them, he came to a flowering plant that was smeared with blood. To Lone Man the plant said, "My Son, you were born from me. I gave birth to you in order that you could go around in the world and do much work" (Bowers 1950: 347). Clearly this tradition asserted the priority of plant persons in relation to Lone Man, the creator figure, and the intentionality concerning bringing forth a world was firmly associated with the purposes of these powerful beings.

After Lone Man created the earth from mud brought up by ducks, he took some of the wood from the trees and fashioned himself a pipe. While he was scattering seeds so that grasses and other plants would grow, Lone Man met a buffalo bull. Even though this animal did not know about his own origins, he clearly had great power; we may even presume that he typified one of those preexisting animals we have encountered in other traditions. Buffalo urinated on a place where the ground had been loosened and told Lone Man, "You can go now but come back when you hear a sound like thunder" (Bowers 1950: 347). When Lone Man heard this sound he returned to that place and found growing there many fine tobacco plants. There were numerous bees buzzing among the blooms of the plants, which was the source of the thunder sound. Buffalo returned and fashioned a tobacco sack from a bladder. Taking tobacco from the sack, Lone Man filled his pipe and pronounced the smoke to be sweet and flavorful.

Lone Man continued to travel with his pipe and finally encountered Coyote or First Man. At first there was tension between these two beings as they argued over which one was the older, that is, which one had the greatest power. A test was proposed that involved how long First Man could lie beside Lone Man's lance; after a very long time, Lone Man returned and found the lance as well as Coyote's bones scattered about. As he was concluding that he was indeed the oldest (most powerful), Coyote jumped up alive. After this convincing demonstration, First Man said, "We will go around the world, and I will help you in everything that you undertake" (Bowers 1950: 348).

The tradition focused particularly on the area of the Missouri River near the mouth of the Heart River where the Mandans had long resided. Lone Man made the land on the east side of the Missouri, and First Man formed the land on the west side; when they were finished, they returned to the area of the Heart River. In another version, when Lone Man returned to the Heart River he noticed a small hill shaped like a heart and said, "This [the hill] was to be the 'Heart of the World,' and this hill is still holy to our people" (Bowers 1950: 35). This tradition clearly casts a symbolic net around a particular place—the Heart River where it emptied into the Missouri. As the Knife River was deeply significant for the Hidatsas and a place where they had long dwelled, so the Heart River became rich in symbolic associations for the Mandans. It was their place; they were put there by their creator; their fundamental identity as a people was interconnected with this land.

It is interesting to compare the earth diver traditions of Northern Plains peoples with traditions developed by the Pawnees, who occupied villages on the Republican River in southern Nebraska and who moved in the late eighteenth century to locations on the Platte River. The Pawnees were Caddoan-speaking people who lived in earth lodge villages, as did the Mandans, Hidatsas, and Arikaras. Along with these people, they had developed a very successful dual economy, depending upon both garden produce and buffalo hunting for their subsistence. The Skidi band of the Pawnees was probably best known for a ritual of human sacrifice, requiring that a young woman be given to the Morning Star (see Dorsey 1907; Linton 1926).

Pawnee origin traditions were as complex and dynamic as those among other peoples, but the core features seem to have been shared very widely. What was striking about these traditions and the ritual processes that embodied them was that the world was sung into being by a chorus of powerful voices (Dorsey 1904b: 5; see also Murie 1984: 43–51). Tirawa was the most powerful of these voices, and it was through his agency that the structure of the world came into being. A complex version of this narrative told by a Pawnee priest named Running Scout provided many rich images (see Dorsey 1904b: 3–14).

Even though many persons knew the main outlines of the origin traditions, individuals who had specialized knowledge, such as Running Scout, were able to provide a wealth of detail that otherwise might not have been available. As is the case with many of these narratives, there was evidence of the influence of contact with missionary Christianity, which is to be expected since this narrative was recorded at the beginning of the twentieth century.

Again, however, it is important to notice that this narrative is not Christian, it is deeply Pawnee.

In this tradition, Tirawa spoke to the other powers by means of Thunder, indicating to them that his intention was to provide a structure to the universe: "Each of you gods I am going to station in the heavens; and each of you shall receive certain powers from me, for I am about to create people who shall be like myself. They shall be under your care. I will give them your land to live upon, and with your assistance they shall be cared for" (Dorsey 1904b: 3). Tirawa then placed Sun and Morning Star in the east and Moon and Evening Star in the west. Sun and Morning Star were male powers while Moon and Evening Star were female powers. Of Evening Star, Tirawa said, "You shall be known as Mother of all things; for through you all beings shall be created" (Dorsey 1904b: 3).

In addition to the placement of these powers, Tirawa commanded North Star to occupy the north and Spirit Star to occupy the south. The four star beings were then assigned the following role: "You four shall be known as the ones who shall uphold the heavens. There you shall stand as long as the heavens last, and, although your place is to hold the heavens up, I also give you power to create people. . . . Your powers will be known by the people, for you shall touch the heavens with your hands, and your feet shall touch the earth" (Dorsey 1904b: 4). Tirawa also placed Black Star in the northeast, Yellow Star in the northwest, and two other (unnamed) stars in the southwest and the southeast. To Black Star was given power to create animals, and "the animal gods were to be given power from the Black Star to communicate with mankind so that people would understand the mysterious powers of the animals" (Dorsey 1904b: 4).

After all of these powers had taken their places and assumed their appointed roles, the stars of the four directions remained with Tirawa. To the powerful female being, Evening Star, Tirawa gave Clouds, Winds, Lightnings, and Thunders. These beings were placed at the edge of Evening Star's garden in the west, and, once they arrived at that location, Tirawa said that they would take the form of human beings. "They shall have the downy feather in their hair. Each shall wear the buffalo robe for his covering. Each shall have about his waist a lariat of buffalo hair. Each also shall wear moccasins. Each of them shall have the rattle in his right hand. These four gods shall be the ones who will create all things" (Dorsey 1904b: 5).

As compared with the other Northern Plains traditions, this version did not portray the origins of the world by means of animal agency, although animals became important for the human beings who were to come. Rather, the tradition represented Tirawa as the most powerful in the array of sky powers. This being "mediated" power to create the world to the stars of the four directions, and the creation took place through the agency of powers who took human shape but who were under the direction of Evening Star.

As indicated above, the emergence of the world arose through song. The scene was filled with complex imagery: the four beings stationed in the west at the edge of Evening Star's garden began to sing and to shake their gourd rattles. As they sang, clouds arose, wind blew in the clouds, and thunder and lightning entered the clouds. At this point Tirawa dropped a pebble into the clouds, and after the storm had passed, there remained a vast expanse of water. When the four singers struck the water with their war clubs, it separated, and the earth appeared. As they began their second song, a great storm arose above the earth, bringing rain and lightning strikes, which gave life to the newly created world. With their third, fourth, and fifth songs the trees and plants came into existence, streams and rivers filled with pure water arose, and seeds were scattered so that other plants would grow on the earth.

After these things had occurred, Morning and Evening Star copulated, and a female child was born. On the occasion of this birth, Evening Star said, "When I give the people buffalo, a female calf shall be born in the wintertime, who shall be a holy calf. The people may kill this female calf, and offer it as a sacrifice, for this buffalo calf will be made a sacrifice, to remind the people that a girl was created first" (Dorsey 1904b: 6). Then Sun and Moon copulated, and a male child was born in the summertime. As a consequence of a sixth and seventh song, the male and female children were transported to the earth on a cloud, and, from these two, all the human beings were born.

Siouan traditions about the origin of the world shared many of the complexities that were evident in the Pawnee narratives. Among the Wahpeton Dakota, who were living near Griswold, Manitoba, in the early part of this century, there was a tradition that featured primal waters (Wallis 1923: 36). A central being, the Great Power, created the earth, humans, and animals for the people to eat. Another being, Spider, also had great powers and claimed to have been the first to be created. A narrative that featured Spider's trickster characteristics occurred in a story about a time when the Indians were near starvation. Spider invited all of the animals to a meeting in a forest; instead of conducting a meeting, however, Spider surrounded the forest with his web, and all the animals were killed by the Indians (Wallis 1923: 65).

In another tradition, the creator told all the animals to assemble for a meeting in order to decide what the human beings who were yet to be created should eat. They discussed the problem, but no solution could be reached until Spider was summoned to the meeting. Spider said that the problem could be solved in the following manner: since all the humans would be mortal, there would always be space for each new generation to exist; but there must be some way, he said, to prevent the humans from killing all the animals and causing widespread starvation. Then Spider "announced his intention of creating marshes, lakes, hills, deserts, as places where people would not be able to live. In such places the animals would have to take up their abode. Though some would be killed for meat, others, and still others, would be born. That is how animal life started. Thus they planned and to this all agreed" (Wallis 1923: 73).

There was also another interesting tradition that focused upon the power of underwater beings, which were viewed as immense and lived in deep bodies of water or in large waterfalls (Dorsey 1894: 438). In some Lakota traditions these powerful beings were portrayed as having brought earth from the underwater world; the narrative then followed a typical Northern Plains pattern—out of this earth the world was formed. There was some evidence also that there were beliefs that identified these great water spirits as male and their female counterparts as spirits that enlivened the earth. Evidently such beliefs informed certain Lakota ritual acts that involved making offerings to the water and to the earth.

One of the more complex versions of the Lakota cosmogony was constructed out of elements of several traditions by James A. Walker, a physician at Pine Ridge who lived among the Lakota from 1896 to 1914 (1983: 206–45). Even though Walker's work has received extensive analysis and criticism, it was constructed on the basis of his thorough knowledge of Lakota traditions (1983: 1–36). While it was presented in a manner that sought to communicate with non-Indians, it is still interesting because it included images and characters that are relevant for understanding the broader symbolic networks within which humans and animals were experienced.[8]

According to the Walker version, the creation of the universe proceeded from a central being and occurred in various stages. This central being was Rock: "Inyan (Rock) had no beginning for he was when there was no other. His spirit was Wakan Tanka (The Great Mystery), and he was the first of the superior gods" (Walker 1983: 206). This oldest being, Rock, was alone, and though he desired to show forth his powers, there was no one to see or acknowledge his greatness. In order to remedy this situation, Rock created from his own substance another creature that took the form of a great disk. "This disk he named Maka (Earth). He gave to Maka a spirit that is Maka-akan (Earth Goddess). She is the second of the superior gods, but she is a part of Inyan" (Walker 1983: 207).

The energy taken for the generation of the earth put such a strain on Rock that he bled profusely, and his blood became the blue waters of the earth. From this blood-water another being separated, becoming the blue dome of the sky. This being was pure spirit compared to the materiality of Rock, Earth, and the waters. He was known as Skan, but he seemed to have emerged through the synthesis of many sky powers: "When these powers assumed one shape . . . a voice spoke, saying, 'I am the source of energy. I am Skan'" (Walker 1983: 207). After the emergence of other aspects of the universe, Skan took aspects of himself, Earth, and Rock and created Sun, who was the fourth great power to emerge.

In this tradition, creation continued to emerge, and, as various powers took their places and began to interact, the universe became more and more complex. At a certain point in this process, Skan assembled all of the powers who had influence below the surface of the earth and announced his intention to create other beings who would serve the will of Wakan Tanka (Walker 1983: 225–26). Skan took from Rock material out of which he created bones, from Earth he took material and made flesh, and out of the waters he created blood. He molded these materials into masculine and feminine shapes and

gave to each animation, intelligence, affections, and the capacity to reproduce. To these beings Skan said, "You and your offspring shall be known as
the Oyate Pte (Buffalo People)" (Walker 1983: 226). They lived underground,
below the level where humans would dwell. At the deep symbolic level, this
part of the tradition powerfully evokes the animal upon which the Lakota
people would depend for food.[9]

The traditions we have studied in this chapter provide essential insight
into Northern Plains understandings of the basic structure of the world as it
was experienced by different peoples. The web of origin traditions constituted a symbolic horizon that informed the consciousness and experience of
particular groups. The figures in these traditions were often subjects of both
allusion and indirect reference as well as specific treatment in narratives about
their exploits. There were some groups, such as the Lakotas, for whom the
deepest knowledge and the most creative telling of these traditions might
have been reserved for experienced narrators or shamans (Walker 1983: 205).
But even in this case, the experience of ordinary persons was affected by the
symbolic forms mediated through the narratives.

It is important to emphasize that these traditions made the point that what
it means to be a human being required that one assume an appropriate relation with the other-than-human powers of the world, including the animals.
Indeed, some traditions seemed to suggest that what it meant to be human
was fundamentally intertwined with a relation to particular places and specific
animals. The symbolic meanings evoked by these traditions constituted a
sacred ecology that infused the everyday world with a dense and complex
horizon of associations. While these traditions were richly textured and constituted the ground for basic attitudes and experiences of the world, there
were other narratives that spoke more concretely about the gift of animals to
human beings for food. These traditions often spoke of a powerful culture
hero who brought the animals to the human beings. Some of these traditions
became texts for important ritual processes that preceded the hunting and
killing of animals. It is the purpose of the next two chapters to explore these
oral traditions and to describe the ritual processes and the understandings of
animal kinship that they so powerfully informed.

the 3 gift of animals

In the origin narratives, the powerful animals that existed before the world was formed seem to be differentiated from animals that Northern Plains peoples encountered in their everyday worlds, animals that they hunted and killed for food. The primal animals of the creation accounts clearly transcended the everyday world of killing and butchering. Some appeared to be powerful spirits who assumed the form of creatures that the people knew and hunted. But even in their animal forms they revealed their true identities as creator and/or trickster figures. Some of them seemed to be spirit animals who possessed self-generating capacities, and their other impressive powers marked them with a special transcendence. Oral performances brought these transcendent persons into the people's present experience, and in rituals they irrupted into their everyday world, constituting an embodied symbolic context that grounded more specific interchanges with game animals encountered on the hunt.[1]

The distribution of knowledge about origin traditions and participation in ritual processes was not the same in all Northern Plains societies. For example, among some groups there were religious specialists, or medicine persons, who had custody of many rituals and traditions. In these cases, the social distribution of detailed knowledge about the origin of the experienced world would be more limited than was the case when religious controls were less restrictive. Generally speaking, the distribution of knowledge about origin traditions was more likely to be less restrictive among groups such as the Blackfeet who had a bilateral kinship system and a mode of transfer of ritual knowledge that was not strictly controlled by consanguinity, while among groups with more cohesive kinship systems, such as the clan structure of the Mandans, there was stricter control of ritual knowledge and its practice and transfer.

There were other animal traditions that were more widely distributed among the people and may have shaped their experience of game animals as much as the origin accounts. For example, oral traditions that dealt with how the people were given animals for food have been recorded for many Northern Plains groups. Though quite diverse, these traditions may be classified into four broad types: those that featured an animal master or mistress, those that focused on the activities of a culture hero, those that focused on kinship between humans and animals, and those that portrayed the gift of animals through the agency of anonymous, often poor, individuals. Again, the boundaries between these types were not impermeable, and two or more types often appeared in the same narrative.

Some of these traditions struggled with a basic dilemma that characterized most Northern Plains hunting societies: among those groups that represented animals as having characteristics analogous to or even identical with those of humans, how were humans to understand what it meant to kill animals and consume their flesh? On the face of it, the tensions were severe: one was eating the flesh of a being like one's self, a person with a kinship network, perhaps a wife and children, a being for whom relatives would grieve. Beliefs that individual animals possessed "souls" that were not destroyed when their bodies were taken for food helped soften the conflicts embodied in this dilemma; even so, the ambiguities were not completely resolved.

Animal Master Traditions

A tradition that included a master of the animals was found among the Cheyennes. This tradition focused upon a figure known as E hyoph sta, Yellow Haired Woman, and was, according to Grinnell, very old. Indeed, he said that the Cheyennes themselves believed that the Yellow Haired Woman tradition was older than the stories about their other culture heroes, Sweet Medicine and Erect Horns (Grinnell 1962: 244). This tradition preserved memories of a time when the people were living to the east of the Missouri River, probably in upper Minnesota. It was a hard time, and the people were very hungry: "They were depending for food on the fish, geese, and ducks in the little lakes, for where the people were camped there was almost nothing to eat" (Grinnell 1962: 245). At that time, the buffalo were unknown.

Facing the prospect of starvation, the chiefs called two young men who were themselves the sons of chiefs and instructed them to go ahead of the people in search of food. Meanwhile, the people had packed all of their belongings on dog travois in preparation to move. The chief's instructions to the young men indicated the desperate condition of the people: "You must try hard. You hear the old people and the children crying for food. Be sure to find something. Do not come back until you do" (Grinnell 1962: 245). The form that this narrative took was widespread (two young men, one older, the other younger, bound together by friendship or kinship), but the content had finally to do with the gift of the buffalo to the Cheyenne people.

The two young men traveled toward the north for eight days and came upon a large mountain. At the foot of the mountain there flowed a river. The two young men were exhausted, nearly starving, and decided to cross the river in order to reach the mountain so that they could die together. As they began to wade the river, something under the water seized the younger man and prevented him from crossing to the other side. The other man went to his friend and shook his hand for the last time. Then "the younger shouted his war cry, and the elder went on weeping toward the bank. He walked out of the water and then up and down the bank crying" (Grinnell 1962: 246).

Suddenly the elder youth saw a strange figure who came out of the mountain and moved down toward him. As he came closer, the young man saw that a coyote skin covered his entire body, including his head. Coyote Man entered the river and with his large knife killed the great water snake that had held the younger man hostage. After killing the snake, Coyote Man told the elder youth to go up the side of the mountain until he reached a rock door. There he would meet an old woman up the mountain side. The youth found the old woman, and she came down with ropes, with which she began to transport the meat back up the mountain. Coyote Man and the older youth carried the younger man, who was exhausted and near death. When they reached the rock door they entered the mountain. On the inside it was shaped like a tipi and had a skin-covered sweat lodge on one side. After heating stones and placing them at the center of the sweat lodge, Coyote Man entered with the younger man. As he sprinkled water on the hot stones, he sang four songs; at the end of this ritual, the younger man regained his strength.

After the old woman had finished feeding meat to the two young men, they looked around the lodge and suddenly saw a beautiful young woman. After some discussion with Coyote Man, who proposed that one of the young men take his daughter in marriage, it was decided that the younger man would perform this role. Then Coyote Man evoked a vision: "After the younger [man] had chosen the young woman for his wife, the coyote man told them to look to the north. They did so, and saw a big field of corn. He told them to look to the east, and there they saw a country covered with buffalo. He told them to look to the south, and they saw elk, deer, and all kinds of game . . . and to the west they saw all kinds of birds" (Grinnell 1962: 248). The vision anticipated the animals that the Cheyenne people would receive as a consequence of this newly established kinship relation.

As represented in this tradition, Coyote Man was clearly neither man nor animal. Rather, he was a transcendent spirit-person who had control of the animals and was willing to grant them as a gift to the people. The mediation of the gift of animals was through the agency of his daughter, Yellow Haired Woman, and the sexual and social relationship that had been established through her with the people. But there were rules that had to be obeyed if this arrangement was to continue. One rule required that Yellow Haired Woman refrain from expressing certain attitudes toward animals: "If ever a little buffalo calf is brought into the camp," Coyote Man said to his daughter, "do not say to it 'My poor animal.' If they ever bring in any kind of fowl, never say to it, 'My poor animal.' *Do not express pity for any suffering creature*" (Grinnell 1962: 249, emphasis added). At first this may seem like a curious taboo, but, given what the Cheyennes believed about animals, it may express some of the layers of ambiguity they felt about killing them for food.

After stopping to rest four times on the way, the two young men and Yellow Haired Woman finally reached the Cheyenne village. The morning after their arrival the camp was surrounded by buffalo, and the people killed as many as they needed. Recognizing the relationship between the appearance of the buffalo and the presence of Yellow Haired Woman, the leaders of the people deliberated about how properly to thank her and what gifts might be provided in exchange for the animals she had brought. In response she said that her father had instructed her not to accept gifts; all she had to do was to be obedient to him, and it would be well with the people.

All did not remain well, however. Yellow Haired Woman and the two young men made a visit to her parents, traveling mysteriously by closing their eyes; when they opened them they were in front of the peak. Even though they were warmly welcomed and feasted, Coyote Man told them to return to their people and not come to his lodge again. He emphasized the rule of no pity once again. After they had closed and opened their eyes, they were back at the village. Four years later Yellow Haired Woman violated her father's taboo, expressing pity for a young buffalo calf that some children were abusing. The consequences were disastrous: "That day the buffalo all disappeared" (Grinnell 1962: 251).

Cheyennes who knew this tradition understood that after Yellow Haired Woman's mistake times were hard for their predecessors until the buffalo were brought back to them. Some Cheyennes believed that their predecessors had gradually forgotten about the buffalo that were given during Yellow Haired Woman's time. These people were represented as living once again in a country to the north, probably upper Minnesota. In this homeland they were again dependent upon fish, birds, and smaller game animals for their food (Grinnell 1972, 2: 339).

Culture Hero Traditions

Two Cheyenne traditions dealt with the reintroduction of the buffalo, one of which was a narrative of two culture heroes and the other of which was a narrative about a single culture hero, Sweet Medicine. The tradition that spoke about two culture heroes is a synthetic narrative that represents the assimilation of two separate peoples to form what became the Cheyenne nation. The Suhtai were a linguistically related group that joined the Cheyennes and contributed the narrative about their own culture hero, Standing on the Ground (also known as Erect Horns as well as a number of other names). Sweet Medicine and Standing on the Ground appeared together in a number of traditions concerning the second gift of buffalo, and Sweet Medicine appeared alone in an additional set of traditions. Both of these streams of tradition were complex: they portrayed two peoples becoming one nation, they embodied memories of Cheyenne migrations, and they spoke at length about how the people received corn and became reacquainted with the buffalo as a food source. Although there were several versions of these narratives, there were common features that were relevant to the second gift of the buffalo to the Cheyenne people.

Many versions of the story of the two young men, Sweet Medicine and Standing on the Ground, included an opening scene where the people were camped in a great circle (Grinnell 1972, 2: 340–45; 1971: 257–63; 1907: 179–94). At the center of the camp a number of people were gathered watching two men playing a game; the people who were watching placed bets on who they thought would win. Two young men appeared from opposite sides of the circle, and as the people watched the game they noticed that both of them were dressed and painted in exactly the same manner. One description of their identical dress and body paint indicated that each was "naked except for his breechcloth, and was painted yellow all over and striped down with the fingers; on his breast was a small circle, in red, and on the back a half moon of the same color. His face under his eyes was painted black, and there was a red stripe around his wrists and ankles; he had a yellow down feather on his scalplock and wore his robe hair side out" (Grinnell 1971: 258). The two young men discovered that each had received instructions about how to dress and paint from the same source, an old woman who lived in a spring that flowed out from under a large rock. They decided to return to the spring, and, upon their arrival, each entered the water and came into the lodge of the old woman, who rose and embraced each of them warmly, addressing them as her grandchildren. She set before the two young men dishes of buffalo meat and corn, which they ate quickly since they were very hungry; even though they consumed a great deal, there was still plenty of food left in the dishes.

After they had finished eating they were repainted by the old woman; each was painted red with yellow sun and moon symbols, their new body paint being a part of their ritual transformation. Then the old woman evoked a vision of the four directions. In one direction they saw a land covered with buffalo, in another direction they saw lush fields of corn, in another direction they saw many horses, in still another direction they saw Indians fighting, and among them they recognized themselves. The old woman assured them that they would always be victorious over their enemies. Then she sent the two young men back to the people with the following instructions: "Say to your people, women and children, and all the bands of the societies, 'We have come out to make you happy; we have brought out something wonderful to give you.' Tell your people that when the sun goes down I will send out the buffalo" (Grinnell 1971: 260). Buffalo came out of the spring during the entire night, and when the sun arose the next morning, the Cheyenne country was covered with these animals.

Clearly the old woman in the spring portrayed by this tradition was a mistress of both the animals and plants. She had the power both to give the buffalo and corn to the people and to withhold these gifts of food. Because of the relationship established between this old woman and the two young men, Sweet Medicine and Standing on the Ground, the power that she possessed became available to the people through the agency of the culture heroes. The old woman clearly performed the same functions for the people as did Coyote Man in the previous tradition. While these traditions are different in their portrayal of the spirit-person who was the master/mistress of the animals, they both lead to the same consequence: the people receive the gift of food.

Both the Sweet Medicine and Standing on the Ground traditions became bearers of symbolic meaning that informed larger ritual processes focused on the renewal of the animals. These rituals are discussed in chapter 5.

The Sweet Medicine tradition appeared in several versions, but they all shared many of the same core meanings. Grinnell recorded two extensive Sweet Medicine narratives and several fragments that contained material that was apparently very old (1908: 271–320). The first of these traditions portrayed Sweet Medicine as an orphan who was cared for by a poor old woman. Despite his marginal circumstances he was a being who possessed more than human powers. Early in his life Sweet Medicine demonstrated this power by cutting off his head with a bow string and then coming back to life.

He also came into conflict with the power structure of Cheyenne society. One day while he was skinning a buffalo, a chief came up to Sweet Medicine and demanded the robe. Even though Sweet Medicine refused, the older man persisted. Finally, Sweet Medicine, in a rage, killed the chief with a buffalo leg bone. After this event, Sweet Medicine was pursued by Cheyenne warriors, but because of his mysterious powers they were not able to capture him. Not only could he move swiftly and cover long distances in what seemed an instant, he was also able to transform himself into an animal or a bird at just the right moment to make his escape.

During the long period when the warriors were pursuing Sweet Medicine, the people moved about the country searching for food, which was in increasingly short supply. These traditions seem to draw a causal connection between the people's inability to recognize who Sweet Medicine was and their increasing desperation for food. Finally they sent word to Sweet Medicine through his brother that he could return. The narrative made clear, however, that this invitation masked the intent to get rid of him, this time through the agency of his own relative.

After Sweet Medicine received the message he returned to the people and entered his brother's lodge where he went to sleep. The next morning his brother asked Sweet Medicine to go hunting and while they were away from the camp, the people moved. The two brothers successfully killed a buffalo and after butchering it the brother asked Sweet Medicine to remain with the meat until he returned with a dog travois to transport the kill to the camp. He gave Sweet Medicine a willow branch to brush the flies off the meat and then departed.

Sweet Medicine had now been abandoned both by his brother, which was a deep violation of primary kinship relations, and by the Cheyenne people as a whole. Again, the tradition draws a connection between this behavior and the people's increasingly desperate situation. Although they had moved about for a year after leaving Sweet Medicine, they found less and less to eat. After the year had passed the people returned to the spot where Sweet Medicine had been abandoned. They found him still guarding the bones of the buffalo that he and his brother had killed.

The path that was worn by his walking had become so deep that Sweet Medicine could not be seen. While he could be heard talking to himself, he would not speak to his brother or his other relatives. Suddenly he disappeared, and the consequences were immediate and disastrous. "The buffalo and all the animals disappeared, and the people began to starve. All that they had to live on were such things as they could gather from the ground. . . . As time went on, they grew more and more hungry; and at last all were becoming so weak that they could hardly travel . . . the people mere skin and bone; and children helpless from starvation, and unable to walk" (Grinnell 1908: 276). Sweet Medicine was gone from the people for four years. During this time he journeyed to a mountain in the Black Hills, where he received additional powers from transcendent beings who lived there.

As he made his way back to his people, Sweet Medicine encountered four young boys who were searching outside the camp for something to eat. The culture hero transformed buffalo chips and snow into meat and fat and fed the young people. As was the case with the food offered by the old woman in the spring, the boys were unable to consume all of the meat and buffalo fat. Sweet Medicine instructed the boys to return to the people and tell them to form their camp in a large circle shaped like a crescent moon with the open end facing toward the east. Within this circle they were told to erect a large tipi, one that required at least two or three regular tipi covers.

After all of these things were done, Sweet Medicine told the people to bring him an old buffalo skull and place it at the center of the camp circle. Sweet Medicine began to sing, and as he sang the buffalo skull grunted and moved toward him. At this point he took the buffalo skull, moved into the large tipi, and continued his singing. After he had been singing for two days and two nights, buffalo were heard in the distance. Then on the morning of the third day, buffalo could be seen here and there around the camp circle. He continued to sing, and on the fourth morning buffalo in great numbers were inside the camp circle, surrounding the tipi from which the songs emanated. Sweet Medicine said to the people, "'Now go and kill food for yourselves, as much as you need. I will sit here and sing, and the buffalo will not run away. You can kill all you want here in the camp.' . . . After he saw that they had enough, he called out to them to stop . . . and those buffalo that were alive, all walked out through the gap in the circle" (Grinnell 1908: 278). This tradition portrayed Sweet Medicine as having power over the buffalo, as a kind of master of the animals. He had caused the buffalo to return to Cheyenne country, and he had brought to the people a ritual that would ensure that they would always have plenty of food. In this case the gift of animals included as well the gift of power over the animals.[2]

There was an interesting Blackfoot tradition that portrayed Old Man as a master of the animals, even though the language and imagery of creation still pervaded the narrative. This tradition opened with a beautiful vision of the relationship between the humans, animals, birds, and Napi. According to this narrative, "All animals of the Plains at one time heard and knew him, and all birds of the air heard and knew him. All things that he had made understood him, when he spoke to them—the birds, the animals, and the people" (Grinnell 1962: 137). While these relations seemed initially to be idyllic, they were soon filled with tension between humans and a primary animal, the buffalo. In those early times "there were buffalo. Now the people had no arms, but those black animals with long beards were armed; and once, as the people were moving about, the buffalo saw them, and ran after them, and hooked them, and killed and ate them" (Grinnell 1962: 140). When Napi saw the humans torn to pieces by the buffalo, he determined to change this fundamental relationship by making the buffalo food for the humans. After he had fashioned bows and arrows, he taught the people how to hunt; and after they had successfully killed buffalo, Old Man taught the people how to butcher with stone knives. After butchering, Napi taught the people how to make and use fire in order to cook the meat that had been provided in the hunt (Grinnell 1962: 140–41).

Now that the people had power over the buffalo, Napi established an additional relationship that dramatically reversed what had been constituted through hunting: the people were now commanded to turn to the animals for power. When they slept, the people dreamed, and in their dreams, power animals appeared. Napi said, "Whatever these animals tell you to do, you must obey them. Something will come to you in your dream that will help you. Whatever these animals tell you to do, you must obey them. . . . Be guided by them. . . . Whatever animal answers your prayer, you must listen to him" (Grinnell 1962: 141). The initial vision of communication and harmony moved through the conflicts involved in killing—first buffalo killing humans and then the reversal—and was surprisingly resolved by reestablishing a relation of human dependence upon powers mediated through animals.

Traditions that involved the reversal of animal and human roles also appeared in Arikara stories narrated by Star and Snowbird (Dorsey 1904a: 39–44). In other Arikara traditions, Mother-Corn was responsible for bringing buffalo to the people (Dorsey 1904a: 36–37). Snowbird's account began with a description of an Arikara buffalo-calling ritual that ended in a very successful hunt. After the hunt, the people were told a story about a village of buffalo people. These people looked human, but they had horns and tails; they performed the same ritual that the Arikaras had just enacted, but in this case it was a ritual that resulted in the killing of people. The humans (rather than the buffalo) lived underground and were periodically led through the trunk of a hollow tree to the surface by an individual named Cut-Nose. Cut-Nose was never harmed, for he was the one who brought the humans to the buffalo. One day a young man came out with the people, but he escaped the buffalo attack; it was through his action that the reversal of roles between humans and buffalo would take place.

After his escape the young man came upon the tipi of a beautiful woman; he entered the tipi and was invited by the woman to sleep with her. When they awoke, the woman promised to communicate knowledge that would save his human relatives. Revealing her true identity, she told the man, "My people are Buffalo, and there is a way for them to become real animals. I selected you to be the one to turn them to buffalo, and then my people will not eat your people any more. My father is the chief of the Buffalo, and I learned by listening how your people can be saved" (Dorsey 1904a: 42). In this tradition, the role reversal took place through the transformation of these animal-humans into animals. Buffalo-Woman told the young man that when this transformation had occurred, the buffalo would eat grass rather than people.

While the buffalo people were preparing to engage in the ritual that preceded their killing of humans, the young man worked quickly to make many bows and arrows to give to his people when they emerged from under the ground. As the people started coming out of the ground, emerging from the hollow tree, the young man armed each human, and, before long, they had killed many of the buffalo. The buffalo-people were routed and fled, but before they ran away they took some of the human flesh and carried it with them under their arms. This human flesh became a part of these people, for as they ran away they were transformed into buffalo.[3] The young man and the Buffalo-Woman returned to the village and became members of the Arikara society.

In another Blackfoot tradition, the animals were portrayed as having disappeared from the plains (Grinnell 1962: 145–48). The people were represented as being in a desperate condition. Fearing starvation, they prayed to Old Man, "Oh, Old Man, help us now, or we shall die. The buffalo and deer are gone. Uselessly we kindle the morning fires; useless are our arrows; our knives stick fast in the sheaths" (Grinnell 1962: 145). In response to their prayers, Old Man set off in search of the animals, taking with him a young man who was the son of a chief. They traveled for many days and subsisted only on roots and berries. Finally, Napi and the young man came upon an isolated lodge that had been pitched on the bank of a stream. In this lodge lived a man, his wife, and their young son.

But because Napi knew that things were not always as they seemed, he and his companion decided to investigate further. They assumed different shapes for this task, Old Man becoming a little dog and the young man becoming a digging stick. When the little boy saw the dog, he immediately wanted to keep it; likewise, when the wife saw the beautiful digging stick, she wanted to possess it. But having more than average powers of discernment, the husband warned them that the dog and the stick were not as they seemed on the surface. Even so, the desires of his wife and young son prevailed, and the husband reluctantly allowed them to keep the dog and stick.

While the family was asleep, Napi and the young man ate some of the meat that the husband had brought into the lodge. Because he was such a successful hunter, they concluded that the husband must be the one (the master of the animals) who kept the animals hidden. The next morning the wife and young son went out to gather roots, taking with them the little dog and the digging stick. After a time they came to the mouth of a cave in front of which stood a buffalo cow. The dog ran into the cave, and the digging stick, moving like a snake, followed. Inside the cave they found "all the buffalo and other game, and they began to drive them out; and soon the prairie was covered with buffalo and deer. Never before were seen so many" (Grinnell 1962: 146–47). Napi and the young man escaped the wrath of the master of the animals by attaching themselves, in their forms of a dog and digging stick, to the body of a large buffalo bull. The stick hid himself in the thick hair of the buffalo's neck, and the little dog held fast to the abdominal hair of the animal; in this manner they rode to safety. When they were far out on the plains, they changed into their "true shapes" and began to herd the animals that had been released toward the Blackfoot camp.

When they arrived near the camp, the people began to drive the buffalo over a low precipice into a corral, but they were frustrated in their attempt by a raven. "Every time a band of buffalo was driven near the pis'kun, this raven frightened them away. Then Old Man knew that the raven was the one who had kept the buffalo cached" (Grinnell 1962: 147).

Again Old Man saw through the situation. He discerned that the raven was "in reality" the man (the master of the animals) whom he and the young man had encountered in the lodge by the stream. Old Man punished the raven by hanging him upside down in the smoke hole of his lodge. After many days, Napi released the raven and told him to assume his "right shape" and return to his wife and child. This tradition clearly showed that while the potency of Old Man was great (he claimed to have made the mountains and the rocks) and his powers of discernment sharp, he and the people lived in a world that was inhabited by many other powerful beings. Even Napi had to negotiate this power-filled universe; in some instances, even he had to employ stealth and trickery in order to overcome these adversaries.

Traditions that represented the gift of the animals to the Mandans and Hidatsas sometimes involved tension and conflict between rival powers. In the last chapter we saw how Lone Man and First Man (Coyote) had created the world, shaping the landforms on either side of the Missouri River. After the human beings were created and the animals and plants were in place, Lone Man decided that he would associate himself more closely with the Mandans. In White Calf's version of the tradition (Bowers 1950: 348–51), Lone Man devised a way to be born into Mandan society. He took the form of kidney fat, which a young Mandan woman ate; she was impregnated by this act, and Lone Man grew in her womb until she delivered and he was born among the people. Though the people noticed that the baby grew rapidly and that when he became a young man he seemed to know many things, still they did not recognize who he was.

While he was living as a Mandan, Lone Man came into conflict with another great person, Hoita (Speckled Eagle), who had power over all of the animals. Hoita was living among the people and was the recipient of many presents, among which was a fine white buffalo robe that caught Lone Man's fancy. In order to secure the robe, Lone Man asked for the help of Thunder, Rain, Whirlwind, and Sun. Thunder and Rain brought a storm that drenched Hoita's lodge and robe, and when he put the white robe out for Sun to dry it, Whirlwind blew it to a village located far to the north. A group of Mandans found the robe and brought it back to their village, but instead of giving it to Hoita they gave the robe to Lone Man. The consequence of this conflict between the sky powers and Lone Man was disastrous for the people: "Hoita was angry and went to Dog Den Butte, taking all the animals with him. He held the animals there" (Bowers 1950: 349).

Interestingly, while Mandan tradition represented Lone Man as the creator of both the human beings and the animals, a great sky being, Hoita, had fundamental power over the animals. Thus the gift of the animals, while it was present initially in the origin accounts, involved greater complexity. Part of this complexity was revealed in narratives that told of how Hoita was finally convinced to release the animals from Dog Den Butte. In this sense, there was a kind of second gift of the animals to the Mandan and Hidatsa people.

Lone Man was aware that the animals had disappeared, but he did not seem to know what to do. A small earth creature, Mosquito Mouse, finally made him understand that "Hoita has every living thing captive inside of Dog Den Butte. You should go there," said the mouse, "to see what you can do to protect your people" (Bowers 1950: 349). Mosquito Mouse also revealed that the secret of Hoita's power was a ritual that he was performing inside the butte. Together they made a plan that would convince Hoita to release the animals, since a famine was already beginning to affect the people. This plan involved tricking Hoita into thinking that a young man who had dressed up like him was actually his "son." Hoita was finally convinced that the young man was telling the truth when he saw what looked like lightning coming from the youth's eyes. In actuality, the "lightning" came from the fireflies Lone Man had placed in the young man's eyes. As a consequence, "Hoita went back to Dog Den Butte and told the animals that they could leave. He sent the black-tail deer to the badlands, the white-tail deer to the timber, the bears to the points in the river, the buffaloes to the flat, and the antelopes to the hills." Then Hoita said, "The Mandan can go out now and find plenty of meat. All the people will be happy. Lone Man and I will work together, for I have a son in that village" (Bowers 1950: 351).

A Hidatsa version of this tradition told by Bear's Arm embodied a contest between First Creator (Coyote) and another powerful sky being (Beckwith 1937: 144–48). In this tradition the sky being was Moon's son, who was married to a chief's daughter. Since the people had no horses and the buffalo were far away, Moon's son set up a hunting camp near the buffalo and pro- vided the hungry people with meat in exchange for corn and tobacco. While he was away hunting, Yellow Dog (Coyote) began singing love songs to his wife. Soon Yellow Dog saw an opportunity, entered the young woman's lodge, and had intercourse with her. When Moon's son returned from hunting, he immediately sensed through her smell that his wife had been unfaithful. Her act so angered him that "he went to the game all over the country and told them to go to Dog Den and he went in there also. He took First Creator with him, because he knew that First Creator would naturally side with the Indian people" (Beckwith 1937: 146).

With the disappearance of the game, the people were in desperate straits for food, and First Creator decided to do something to help. He instructed Yellow Dog to scatter buffalo dung on the ground, and, as he did so, buffalo appeared for the people to kill. Even though Moon's son had sought to punish the people for his wife's unfaithfulness, his plan was frustrated by First Creator's powers. The outcome of this contest between the sky powers and First Creator was the release of the animals from Dog Den. After this event, Moon's son did not return to his wife or her people but went instead back to the sky country to live with Morning Star.

Animal Wives and Husbands

Another Mandan tradition related by Ben Johnson (Beckwith 1937: 155–61) involved a widespread motif that we have already encountered on the Northern Plains, the establishment of kinship between humans and animals through marriage. This tradition spoke of a family of six: four buffalo, their mother, Corn Woman, and a younger brother named Magpie. This tradition gathered together symbolic layers having to do with plants and animals and attributed significant power and agency to the youngest and smallest member of the family, Magpie, who was, importantly, a creature who flew above the earth. The four buffalo brothers were known as Fall, Winter, Spring, and Summer, and they brought the buffalo close to the villages during the four seasons of the hunting year.

Magpie had foreknowledge of a flood that was soon to cover the village, but the buffalo brothers would not listen to his warning. They observed that plenty of flesh food was available to the people as a consequence of their yearly activities and that their mother, Corn Woman, was able to supply the people with an abundance of corn to eat. Leaving the buffalo brothers and their mother behind, Magpie and a few others moved toward the Missouri River and continued to the south until they came to Bird's-Bill-Butte, where they established another village.

After some time, Magpie decided to fly back to his previous home to see if any were left alive in the village. As he approached the village, he saw his four buffalo brothers standing on top of their lodge, the water surrounding them as far as one could see. Their mother was in a food cache under the floor of the lodge; she had taken the form of an ear of corn but was still alive. Magpie rescued his mother from the food cache by means of a snare that he wove from the hair of one of his brothers; when Corn Woman jumped out of the food cache, Magpie captured her and pulled her to safety. Then she was tied to the head of one of her sons so that she would be safe during their journey to the newly established village.

All four buffalo brothers started out swimming toward the distant land, and Magpie flew above them, giving them words of encouragement from time to time. Summer Buffalo was the first to become tired and said to Magpie, "Brother, I am exhausted; I shall sink here. This shall mark the distance to which you shall bring out your people to hunt [in the summer]" (Beckwith 1937: 157). The three who were left swam on for a time, and then Fall Buffalo became exhausted and sank. The remaining two swam toward the bluffs of the Missouri River, which had come into view, but before reaching land, Winter Buffalo sank below the surface of the water. Even though Spring Buffalo was within clear sight of the bluffs, he too became exhausted. Magpie caught him by the hair of his head and dragged him the remainder of the distance, finally reaching the southern bank of the Missouri River. Corn Woman was tied to the head of Spring Buffalo, and, "having regained strength, Buffalo and Corn took again the forms of persons and came to Magpie's village and lived there" (Beckwith 1937: 158).

For a time Spring Buffalo lived contentedly in his brother's village. He grew increasingly restless, and one day he smelled corn roasting in the northeast and set off in the direction of the inviting odor. Finally he came to a large village, and, taking the form of a very handsome young man, he entered the village and stood on top of the lodge of a chief who had four wives. Seeing the young man, the husband asked the youngest of his wives to invite the guest in for a meal. Spring Buffalo ignored the requests of the first three wives, but when the fourth wife waved spotted eagle feathers over his head, he immediately entered the lodge. Inside the lodge was a fifth person, the chief's sister, a beautiful young woman named Corn Silk.

The chief and Spring Buffalo became friends, and as their relationship developed the chief offered his new friend, who was of marriageable age, the choice of the women of the village. After the eligible women of the village had tried but failed to attract Spring Buffalo, he said to the chief that of all the women in the village he preferred Corn Silk. The chief agreed to the marriage between Spring Buffalo and his sister. As a consequence of this new relationship, Spring Buffalo reciprocated by bringing the people a very important gift.

The next day . . . he [Spring Buffalo] found buffalo dung and scattered it all about and the next morning the people saw a herd of buffalo on the outskirts of the village. The chief had the announcer cry the hunt, a party was formed and away they went. He now let his name be known as Spring Buffalo and drew the herd in, so the hunt was a success. They came home with plenty of meat. From that time he drew in the buffalo from time to time and as this had not been done before he was looked upon with honor. (Beckwith 1937: 161)

It is important to emphasize that this tradition associated at the symbolic level different layers of reality that were populated by beings possessing diverse powers. The buffalo brothers seem to have been spirits who took animal form. They also were masters of the animals since they were able to call the buffalo and bring them close to the villages. Magpie was associated with sky powers, as was the eagle whose feathers one of the wives used to bring Spring Buffalo into the lodge. Earth powers were present through Corn Woman, and the power of water was pervasive in this narrative. These associations formed horizons of meaning that would have resonated in the experience of people who knew the traditions.

A Lakota tradition narrated by Left Heron established a kinship relationship between human beings, buffalo, and corn (Walker 1983: 109–18). This tradition featured the actions of an unnamed young man who left on a hunting trip, traveling to the west, and did not return to his family; as time passed, he was given up for dead, and his family entered a stage of mourning. After a long time had passed, two people were seen approaching the Lakota camp. It was the young hunter and a beautiful young woman who had long black hair and large nostrils. The man's older sisters were pleased that he had brought this beautiful woman to the camp. After being told that the beautiful woman would have an especially close relationship with the older sisters, the younger sisters were saddened. In response to their distress, the young man went east and soon returned with a yellow-haired woman who became a sister to the younger women.

The hunter and his two wives lived happily together, and in time both gave birth to male children, but the birth circumstances demonstrated that the mothers were clearly not human. When the black-haired wife was about to deliver, the young man's father saw her leaving the camp, traveling toward the west. He climbed up on a hill to watch and saw a female buffalo give birth to a buffalo calf; soon the black-haired woman returned to the camp with a baby boy. When the time for the yellow-haired woman's delivery approached she left the camp and traveled toward the east. Again the boy's father watched from the top of a hill. The yellow-haired woman was surrounded by a whirlwind. After the wind had passed she had a small plant growing beside her, but when she returned to the village she brought a baby boy.

After they became older the two brothers enjoyed playing games together. One day as they were throwing spears into the web of a rolling hoop, the yellow-haired woman's son accidentally hit the buffalo woman's son with his spear. As a consequence of this incident, the relationship between the two mothers became tense; finally the buffalo woman took her son and left the camp, traveling toward the west. Once she was out on the plains she became a buffalo cow and was seen by the husband's father running toward the west with a buffalo calf beside her. Saddened by their sudden departure, the husband determined to follow them and bring back his son.

Before he left, the yellow-haired wife made him four specially painted arrows, tied an eagle feather in his hair, and promised him the protection of the whirlwind during the course of his journey. The buffalo wife and her son traveled faster than human beings, and the young man was only able to follow them because he had the power of the whirlwind and of the painted arrows. He shot one of the arrows in the air, and it followed buffalo woman; then when he became tired or out of breath he called on the whirlwind, and it refreshed him. Finally they reached a mountain range far to the west, and together they entered a cave that led to an underground nation of buffalo people.

The buffalo people were oppressed by an old woman and her husband, Crazy Buffalo. The buffalo wife was the daughter of these two individuals. In a series of contests with these powerful people, the young man was able to use the power of his arrows and the whirlwind to kill Crazy Buffalo and his wife. Even though he had killed his son's grandparents, the buffalo people were very happy and implored the young man to remain with them. He replied that he had responsibility for another wife and son and that, as a hunter, he was also responsible for providing food for his parents and family. After a series of negotiations between the young man and a buffalo-shaman, it was decided that "the buffalo people would lead the buffalo near his father's tipi so that his people would have an abundance of meat" (Walker 1983: 117). The young man agreed to remain with the buffalo people and his buffalo son returned to the camp to be with the yellow-haired woman and her son.

But the arrangement was not to be. The yellow-haired woman had become very sad at the loss of her husband; she became despondent, refusing all offers of comfort, including food and drink. She became very weak and, before she died, told the people "of the young man and how he had found her . . . and taken her for his woman and . . . of his love for little children and how he stayed with the buffalo people so that his people might have an abundance of meat. She said that all must mourn for him as for the dead and that when she cut her yellow hair in mourning, she would wither and die but because she also loved little children, she too would provide food for the people" (Walker 1983: 117). After she cut her hair, the woman died. According to her instructions, the young man's father cut up her body and planted the pieces in the ground. After a nourishing rain, "the bits grew, at first, like rushes, and then large with a yellow top like the hair of the woman. The seed came on the rushes where a woman's breasts should be and it was like milk. Then it hardened and became corn" (Walker 1983: 117–18). The yellow-haired woman had fulfilled her promise to provide the people with food.

Animal wives appeared in additional Northern Plains traditions, indicating that a long process of cultural interchange had taken place among the peoples who lived in this area (see Walker 1983: 392–93, n. 10). While there were often similarities among these traditions, they were usually distinguished by being integrated into particular cultural contexts; in this manner, they became part of a specific people's symbolic heritage. An examination of some of these traditions demonstrates these similarities and differences, as well as providing a more complex understanding of how Northern Plains groups understood their relationships with animals.

An Assiniboine tradition portrayed a man receiving power from Big-Eagle, who was the chief of all the eagles (Lowie 1909: 195–97). As was characteristic of many of these traditions, this narrative began with a conflict between a human and transcendent sky powers. The unnamed man in the narrative was collecting eagle feathers from young birds when he was attacked by their father. He killed the father but was pursued by the chief of the eagles, Big-Eagle. The master of the eagles took the man to a high ridge, where he left him for many days. The man was near starvation when Big-Eagle returned and gave him four of his wing feathers. These would provide power over the buffalo.

The man met two buffalo who threatened his life but who were pacified when he offered them an eagle feather. The second buffalo told the man that he should proceed to a spring where he would find a buffalo cow. When he reached the spring the man spoke to the buffalo cow, who responded by proposing that he return to her camp and become her husband. When he reached the camp the buffalo gave him some kidneys to eat. These organs were from the body of the second buffalo the man had met on the trail; this animal was the brother of the buffalo woman he had married. Thus the human ends up eating his brother-in-law's kidneys. Even though he had eaten a part of one of his relatives, the relationship between the man and his buffalo wife ensured the Assiniboines success in hunting.

After some time, the man married a second wife, a moose-woman, and his buffalo wife gave birth to a child. They were living peacefully together in an Assiniboine camp until the man's brother, Magpie, began to look with lust at moose-woman and to scheme about ways to get her for himself. While his brother was away hunting, Magpie proposed a race between the two wives. In the first contest, buffalo-woman won the race, but in the second contest moose-woman made a mud hole in which buffalo-woman became stuck.

Buffalo-woman was so angry because moose-woman had unfairly won the contest that she took her child and returned to her people.

When the man returned from his hunt and found that one of his wives had gone, he set out toward the buffalo village, intending to bring her back. After he reached the village the buffalo gathered for a great dance; in the course of the dance, the man was trampled to death. Meanwhile, back at the Assiniboine village, Magpie had been living with moose-woman. When his brother did not return, Magpie decided to search for him. When he came to the buffalo village, he found out through his brother's child what had happened. Magpie found a bit of his brother's hair and restored him to life, indicating again the superior power of the sky people.

In another version of this tradition (Lowie 1909: 197–98), Magpie had married a buffalo and a moose. The same conflict ensued between the two wives, and the buffalo-woman and her child returned to her father's village. When she reached the village, buffalo-woman told her father what had happened and how unhappy she had become. When Magpie reached the village he was at first afraid to approach his father-in-law, but finally he worked up the courage to come into his lodge. The old buffalo said that they were about to have a war dance and that Magpie should prepare himself to participate. Magpie replied that he was hungry, and his father-in-law said that he would give him something to eat. In what turned out to be an ominous sign, "he [the father-in-law] allowed him to eat one of his brothers-in-law, but ordered him not to cut his legs and to pile up the meat after skinning him. After the man had eaten, the dance began. They danced three times without hurting him, the calf dancing beside his father. The fourth time all the buffalo jumped up, hooked him, threw him continually in the air, and killed him" (Lowie 1909: 197). The tradition ends with Magpie's brother restoring him to life.

Two Pawnee traditions beautifully illustrate the relationships that could emerge when kinship between humans and animals was established through marriage. One tradition, narrated by Enemy-Fed-Well, described the relationship between a young Pawnee man and his two wives, one of whom was a deer and the other of whom was a buffalo (Dorsey 1904b: 280–83). The young man in this tradition was the son of a chief, but, strangely enough, he did not like women. Even though his family urged him to marry, and many young women came to his lodge, he refused to respond and rejected all of them.

To the east of the Pawnee village there was a deer village, and many of the deer-people knew that the young man was not attracted to human women. One of the deer-women heard about this and decided to try to attract the young man with her flute. She transformed herself into a human and moved to a place near the village, where she began to play her flute. The chief's son followed its sound to where the young woman was sitting, but when he reached her, he did not see a flute. This happened two more times, and on the fourth time the young man finally caught the deer-woman playing the flute.

The young man took her home as his wife, and in a few months the deer-wife gave birth to a baby boy. The deer-wife and her son convinced the young man that he should go to the village of the deer-people and meet his new relatives. All in the deer village were happy to see the deer-wife and her young son, and they warmly welcomed the young husband. In the course of their visit, deer, elk, and antelope instructed the young man and transferred to him some of their powers. Then the deer-wife, deer-boy, and young husband returned with these powers to the lodges of his people.

After he had returned to the Pawnee village, the young man decided to go on a hunt. He traveled far to the west and finally came upon a mysterious tipi that had been erected on the banks of a river. Although he was curious he did not enter the tipi but returned to his people. The next day he went hunting in the west, and again he came upon the same tipi. This time a voice said from within, "Come in, do not stand outside" (Dorsey 1904b: 282). He entered the lodge and encountered a beautiful woman who was clothed in a finely tanned buffalo robe. He stayed with this buffalo-woman and had intercourse with her; as a result of this union, a little buffalo-girl was born.

When his deer-wife found out about his relationship with the buffalo-woman she was very angry. She gathered her people, and they went to the place where the tipi had stood. When they arrived, they saw many buffalo. The buffalo and deer began to fight while the two wives disparaged each other with hateful words. The conflict was not resolved, and finally the buffalo-people withdrew and went to live in a place to the northwest while the deer-people went to a place in the southeast. Even though he had a buffalo-wife and child, the young man decided to go and live with the deer-people. He and his deer-wife returned to his Pawnee relatives when they were of advanced age; they taught the people deer songs and other rituals that had to do with deer power. But the people were, according to this tradition, related by marriage to both the deer and to the buffalo, and the buffalo-girl brought good things to the people as well. "The buffalo-girl is the one who leads all the buffalo around . . . and they follow her . . . this calf led the buffalo to the village of the people, so that the people killed many buffalo" (Dorsey 1904b: 283).

Another tradition, narrated by Wonderful-Sun, focused upon a young man who had received power from the wind (Dorsey 1904b: 284–93).[4] As in the previous tradition, this young man did not express interest in human women even though he was very handsome and a successful warrior. One day when he was out alone he came upon a buffalo cow who had become mired in deep mud. Feeling attracted to her, the young man took off his clothes and had intercourse with the buffalo cow. When he had finished, he tied a shell gorget around one of her horns, and the buffalo cow freed herself from the mud and ran away. About a year passed, and the buffalo cow gave birth to a male calf. The calf was somehow different and was not accepted by the buffalo people. "None of the bulls claimed him. They called the calf 'Man-Straight-Up.' When the calf played with the rest of the young calves they said: 'Go away from us! Your father is not here'" (Dorsey 1904b: 285). Even though the mother was distressed by the rejection of her son, she told him that the reason she had become related to the humans was because "your grandfather wanted smoke and presents from those people [the humans], and the only way to get them was to send one of us to them to have connection [intercourse], so that the two kinds of people would be brought together. You see I was selected to go and stay with this man. Our people especially liked the soul of your father, for he is a good man. He has powers from the gods in the north. The god whose name is 'Standing-Wind' gave him power to do wonders" (Dorsey 1904b: 285).

The buffalo cow took her son and went to the Pawnee village in search of her human husband. They came to the village in human form, "a lovely woman and a lovely boy" (Dorsey 1904b: 285). The boy approached his father several times, but his father refused to recognize him as his son. Exasperated and angry, the buffalo woman finally sent the gorget with the boy and told him to remind his father of the time when he had intercourse with a buffalo cow. Upon seeing the gorget and hearing the story, the man recognized his son, but it was too late, and the next thing he saw was a buffalo cow and calf running toward the hills outside the village.

The man followed his buffalo-wife and son to their people's village, where he was met initially with a threatening reception. He was put to a number of tests that involved distinguishing his wife and son from other buffalo as well as engaging in races with young buffalo bulls. He was able to identify his wife and son, and he used his power from Standing-Wind to defeat the young bulls, but still his life was in danger. Finally the buffalo surrounded the man and charged him from all sides, seeking to kill him, but after the dust had cleared, the man still sat unharmed on the ground. After this test, the man was accepted by the buffalo, and it was decided that he would be transformed into one of them. The buffalo breathed on him, rubbed him, urinated near him, and rolled him in a buffalo wallow.

> Presently he was . . . trying to bellow like a buffalo. Now he felt he was becoming one. He could feel the horns coming out on him, and afterwards he knew he had a buffalo head. The buffalo saw it, and made haste in their work, tumbling him over and over in the buffalo-wallow. Then he stood on his four legs and was a complete buffalo. . . . The calf of course was with him all the time. He was now proud. He could go and play with the other bull-calves, for now his father was not a straight-up-being any more. (Dorsey 1904b: 290)

The chief of the buffalo was getting old, and he decided to send the buffalo family back to the Pawnees with a request for the gifts that had initially been anticipated when the buffalo cow was sent to have a sexual encounter with a human. The buffalo family traveled toward the Pawnee village, and when they were close they transformed themselves into humans. The young man told his people that the buffalo nation wished to receive presents consisting of eagle feathers, black cloth, blue beads, and tobacco. If these presents were sent and received, then the young man said that the buffalo would agree to send food to the people. The people agreed, and the buffalo family traveled again to the buffalo village, bearing the gifts from the human beings.

The gifts were accepted, and the buffalo bulls decided to send a herd to the Pawnees. The herd was led to the village by the father and his buffalo-calf son. The man entered the village and told the people to kill all they wanted but to be sure always to allow his son to escape since it was he who led the herds to the village. "Every few days people saw the buffalo coming with the calf in the lead. They killed and brought meat home. They were very thankful" (Dorsey 1904b: 292). Life was good for a long time until the day when the man who had married the buffalo had intercourse with another woman. As a consequence, she left him and took her people with her. The people were hungry for many years afterward until they made presents to the buffalo calf, which reconciled them with the buffalo people.

> So it was allowed by the buffalo bulls that the people should kill buffalo. Had the boy gone home [to his father] and turned into a human being, then the buffalo would have disappeared. But the boy was there and was between [a mediator] the people and the buffalo. So the spirits of the people and the spirits of the buffalo were on the boy. So the prayer and presents of the people were carried to the buffalo by the boy, and the boy also led the buffalo to the people. (Dorsey 1904b: 292–93)

Animal Adoptions

In addition to establishing relations between human beings and buffalo by means of sexual unions that involved transfers of power and permission to slaughter the buffalo, there were traditions that described the adoption of humans by animals. Among the Blackfeet there was such a tradition (Wissler and Duvall 1908: 121–25); other versions may be found among the Gros Ventres (Kroeber 1907: 94–97) and the Crows (Simms 1903: 290–94). On the Northern Plains the practice of adoption was a long-standing means of establishing relationships both between individuals and among groups. While this practice was known among anthropologists as "fictive kinship," this label sometimes obscures the social realities such as kinship obligations that the practice encouraged.

The Blackfoot tradition portrayed a chief's daughter who was very beautiful but who refused all offers of marriage. Although she was a virgin, she somehow became pregnant, bringing shame both to her and to her family. When the time came for her to deliver, she went alone to a place outside the camp; there she gave birth to a baby boy. Before returning to her people, the young woman buried the child in the ground. After she had departed, four buffalo bulls (the other traditions spoke of seven bulls) came upon the place where the child was buried. They brought the baby back to life, hooked him four times until he became full grown, and adopted him as their own. The bull-fathers told the young man to go for a visit to his people and then return to live with them.

On the way to the Blackfoot camp, the young man had many adventures. While he was traveling he received power from Rabbit and Hawk. These powers enabled him to defeat the power of a buffalo bull who had chased him and tried to kill him. After the bull was defeated, the young man traveled for many days until "he found the four buffalo-bulls that adopted him. They told him that they would take him to their home. They told him that the buffalo had a big cave near the mountains, and that this cave was another country where all the buffalo lived, had lodges, and became as human beings, just like his own people. They told him that when the buffalo came out of the cave they would be buffalo, but that when they went in they became as people" (Wissler and Duvall 1908: 123). The young man entered the cave and found there that all was as his fathers had said: people were living in fine lodges in the midst of a beautiful land.

The buffalo people were under the leadership of a chief who had a very beautiful wife. The chief was so jealous that he threatened to kill any person who so much as looked at his wife. The young man made the mistake of gazing at her and came into immediate conflict with the husband. The four bull-fathers who had adopted the young man fought the chief first, but all were killed. Then the young man turned himself into a buffalo bull and fought the chief until he killed him. After the death of their chief, the buffalo people turned to the young man for leadership. Speaking with authority, "the young man told them that he wanted all of them to go out of this place, never to return again, and that they would be buffalo from then on and never like people again. Then he drove them all out and went to his own tribe" (Wissler and Duvall 1908: 124).

After the young man returned to his Blackfoot kin he began to demonstrate his powers, providing food for an old couple by transforming parts of his clothing into buffalo flesh. The chief of the people observed the young man's power and wished to have him as his son-in-law; he sent his younger daughter to the man, and they were married. After they had been married for some time, the young man told his wife, "'Go ask your father to tell the people to get ready and go out to the lines, for I shall make a buffalo-drive.' . . . So all the people went out to the lines and waited for him. The young man was not gone very long when they saw a great herd of buffalo falling over into the enclosure. After everybody got through butchering, they went home" (Wissler and Duvall 1908: 124–25). So the power mediated by Rabbit and Hawk, as well as the power he had acquired from being adopted by the buffalo, was made available to the Blackfeet through establishing another kinship relation, brought into being by the marriage between the young man and the chief's daughter.

Anonymous Youths

There were other traditions that told how the people acquired power over the buffalo through the agency of young boys, some of whom were anonymous and some of whom were represented as being the sons of chiefs. A representative Pawnee tradition, narrated by Curley-Head, dealt with an anonymous young boy who was a very skillful buffalo hunter (Dorsey 1904b: 109–11). His constant slaughter of the buffalo angered these people because he often left the meat to rot on the plains. The buffalo sent two young female calves who turned themselves into young girls to try to persuade the boy to come with them, and after refusing several times he agreed to go.

When they reached the buffalo village the animals took the boy and put him on a high hill that rose from the middle of a great body of water. He stayed on the top of the hill without food or water for many days, crying for power to help him. Birds, including hawks, eagles, and buzzards, took pity on the young man and helped him escape from the mountain top. The birds had given the boy their power, including the ability to transform himself into a bird, and the buffalo were finally defeated. After this time the people were able to kill many animals. In a tradition narrated by Yellow-Calf (Dorsey 1904b: 111–14) the young boy who was the central character obtained similar power over the buffalo. Indeed, the buffalo became so plentiful that "people did not have to go hunting, for the buffalo came in large droves, and the people killed them. The people had so much dry meat and corn that they had to dig cellars in the ground to put their meat and corn in" (Dorsey 1904b: 114).[5]

Many of the oral traditions examined in this chapter struggled with the issue of how the people were related to the animals upon which they were dependent for food and other useful items, such as lodges and clothing. However this struggle was resolved (and we have seen that there were several alternative solutions), these traditions provided an additional symbolic layer that gave shape to the way Northern Plains peoples experienced their worlds. These traditions clearly enabled Northern Plains peoples to sustain a complex sense of their relation to the animals they killed. Through marriage and sexual union, human beings achieved a kind of double consciousness that enabled them to empathize with both human and animal realities and envision interchanges in their destinies.

A comparative example of such double consciousness appears in a hunting tradition on the Labrador Peninsula; this tradition, which portrayed a young man who married a caribou woman (Tanner 1979: 136–37), sheds further light on the narratives examined in this chapter. As a consequence of his union with a caribou woman, the young man could view reality from the perspective of both the human hunter and the caribou. Because of this change in perspective, the young man understood that when they hunted, his human relatives saw caribou trying to escape, observed them being shot and falling to the ground, saw them bleed and finally die. But from a caribou perspective he saw the animals as persons, living in family groups and hunting in much the same way as humans. When one of their members was pursued by human hunters, the young man saw a person clad in a white cape, running away, trying to make an escape. When this person was shot, the young man saw his relative throw off the cape and continue to run to safety. Rather than a person running away, the human hunters saw a caribou; and rather than a white cape that was left behind, the hunters saw the carcass of a dead animal.

A similar tradition told by Yup'ic Eskimo hunters also illustrates this point (Fienup-Riordan 1994: 3–4). This tradition tells of the experience of a young boy who went to live with the seals. During this time the boy stayed in a communal house "where an adult bearded seal hosted him and taught him to view the human world from the seals' point of view" (Fienup-Riordan 1994: 3). This communal house had a skylight through which the boy could observe the human beings going about their daily activities. From the seal perspective, humans were behaving appropriately when they kept their doorways clear of snow, their village clean, and their minds clear. Through these acts, they prepared the way for the seals to enter the human world and become food. Because the seals could always observe the human world, they knew whether the hunters had behaved in an appropriate manner. And like the caribou people, the seals did not die when they were taken for food. Rather, they were regenerated again and again, maintaining the endless cycle of reciprocity between humans and animals.

The traditions dealt with in this chapter provided symbolic layers that enabled Northern Plains peoples to imagine how, at some time in their past, they received the gift of animals. Animals were assigned a status in social reality that provided support for the necessary hunting and killing of them that occurred in these societies. Clearly these traditions were products of the religious imagination, as were the creation accounts, and they were very richly imagined. They provided a complex context for understanding human-animal relationships, and some of these traditions informed the ritual processes that surrounded hunting. These rituals are the subject of the next chapter.

animal

rituals
on the

northern

plains

4

The last two chapters discussed the primacy of animals in the religious imagination of Northern Plains peoples. Whether they were interpreted as spirits who took the form of animals or as humans becoming interchangeable with animals, animal figures appeared frequently in Northern Plains oral traditions. The rituals that are the subject of this chapter deepen the sense in which animals were primary in Northern Plains experience. It was in ritual enactments, for example, that animal figures were inscribed on objects such as tipis and drums, and it was in ritual enactments that animal voices and movements were expressed in dance and song. Even though several animals in the Northern Plains environment appeared in these traditions and ritual processes, the buffalo was the most important food animal. The hunting rituals examined in this chapter all focus upon enactments that provided Northern Plains peoples access to this great animal.[1] These rituals were clearly informed by the intention either to capture animals for food or to acquire their power for other purposes, such as healing or success in war. In this sense, Northern Plains animal rituals formed a deep layer of practice that was essential to the people's lives. These practices were informed by complex meanings embedded in shared cultural symbols mediated in oral narratives. These traditions often provided an account of the origin of a ritual and formed a kind of "text" that guided the enactment of the ritual.[2]

As complex enactments, there were several interrelated elements that characterized the hunting rituals themselves.

1. The timing of a ritual was sometimes determined by an individual's decision to sponsor it and sometimes because the time was right in the ritual calendar.
2. Rituals usually required the construction of a special structure, or they occurred in a structure that had been constructed for other ritual purposes. These structures sometimes had a special shape and often an area that functioned as an "altar."
3. Special clothing and ritual objects such as arrows and pipes were gathered or constructed for specific rituals. In hunting rituals, as well as other enactments, the use of animal body parts such as the skull, neckbone, spinal column, hoof, scrotum, and hide was very common; the use of bird feathers and body parts was widespread as well.
4. The application of appropriate body paints, often by persons who were religiously qualified to perform this task, was a necessary aspect of most rituals.
5. The sweat lodge accompanied important ritual processes.
6. Smoking and smudging with sweetgrass or sage were characteristic of most rituals.
7. Dances that embodied animal movements and animal voices were essential features of most hunting rituals.
8. Ritual sexual intercourse as a means of acquiring or transferring power was present among some groups on the Northern Plains.
9. Northern Plains societies almost always had some degree of religious specialization, which meant that there were ritual leaders in charge of the enactment. For example, vision experiences that gave rise to a

bundle or ritual process usually included songs and other specialized knowledge. The right to sing the songs and to manipulate special knowledge was sometimes confined to the practice of those individuals who were defined as medicine persons.

10. Women often played a central role in hunting rituals and sometimes had their own dances.

While not all of these elements appeared in every hunting ritual presented in this chapter, a good number of them are evident.

In a ritual process there was also the requirement that the songs, dances, and gestures be done according to the pattern that was communicated in the oral traditions that gave rise to the practice. Those with special ritual knowledge and experience were in a position not only to judge the correctness of ritual action but also to reinterpret ritual processes. The reinterpretation of rituals at critical points in the experience of Northern Plains peoples enabled them to survive the maelstrom of social change imposed by conquest and confinement to reservations.[3]

Another distinction that characterized ritual processes generally and hunting rituals specifically was the difference between the individual and the group. If power was granted to an individual in a vision, then the power associated with this personal experience might be embodied in a specific ritual process, including perhaps particular movements and songs. Also involved might be the use of a bundle composed of objects revealed in a vision such as bones, feathers, pipes, and other items that were gathered together and wrapped in an animal skin. The power of the vision embodied in the bundle and ritual process might initially be effective primarily for the individual, benefiting this person and perhaps his or her family. But most hunting bundles and their associated ritual processes were finally believed to benefit the people as a whole.

When the ritual objects enfolded in bundles were enacted in song, movement, and dance, the human participants were not simply playing a role, as in a drama, although the rituals were often visually quite spectacular. At a deeper level there was the belief that those who enacted the ritual became identified with the power of the animal persons, spirits, or culture heroes who were responsible for the original gift to the people. Through ritual transformation, these humans released the energies associated with the bundle or ritual into the present, infusing the everyday world of hunters with transcendent significance and assuring that the purpose of the ritual would be fulfilled.

In addition, the bundles that were central to many ritual processes were believed to be "alive" in the sense that they embodied the energies associated with the founding predecessors, whether human or animal. In hunting bundles, these powers usually had a fundamental association with animal body parts. When the oral tradition represented an animal or bird giving a body part or skin to a bundle, then the specific power associated in the tradition with that gift was believed to be present in the animal skin or body part that was acquired for the construction of the bundle. These powers were made active in the everyday world through ritual manipulation of the items in the bundle. Even when not in use, bundles still embodied power, were believed to be alive, were treated with respect, and were often surrounded by complex requirements for their care as well as restrictions on their owners.

Among the Blackfeet, as well as other groups on the Northern Plains, bundles were often owned by individuals. Sometimes they were strictly personal, having arisen as a consequence of a vision in which an individual was granted specific hunting powers. The bundles discussed in this chapter were usually represented as having arisen in the experience of either a predecessor or contemporary, but they were viewed as having benefit not only for the individual and his or her family but for the group as well. Ownership of these bundles, especially among the Blackfeet, could be transferred to another individual, and there were complicated rituals associated with the transfer of the larger, more complex bundles.

Among the village societies, such as the Mandans, ownership was clan-based, although an individual was responsible for the care of the bundle. These bundles tended to be associated with particular villages, as they were among the Pawnees, who were prevented from marrying outside their village. For this reason, even though an individual might be responsible for its care, the bundle was associated with the group and remained within the village (Murie 1984: 7). Transfers in these societies were usually within the kin group, while among the Blackfeet transfers could occur between individuals who were not related by blood.

An extended analysis of hunting rituals on the Northern Plains provides us with a deeper and more complex understanding of how the religious dimensions of these cultures, which condensed in ritual symbols, constituted the way the people related to the animals that were hunted and killed for food. We will begin the analysis with hunting bundles among the Blackfeet.

The Blackfeet had a small hunting bundle called the *iniskim* (buffalo rock) that was represented in some traditions as arising through the vision experiences of a woman (Wissler 1912: 242–45).[4] These bundles were widely distributed, indicating that the experience of finding such rocks, which were often interpreted as having an animal shape, was not limited to a few individuals. Even though owned by individuals, the traditions that told of these bundles' origin represented the iniskim as having benefit for all Blackfeet.

One origin tradition focused on the vision experiences of a poor individual named Weasel-Woman (Wissler and Duvall 1908: 85–87). She was out one day looking for wood when she heard a strange sound. At first she thought it came from the wing movements of a large bird, but she saw no hawk or eagle nearby. Then she heard what sounded like a voice, but she could not understand what was being said. Finally, the voice became clearer. It was singing:

Yonder woman, you must take me.
I am powerful.
Yonder woman, you must take me.
You must hear me.
Where I sit is powerful.
        (Wissler and Duvall 1908: 85)

Looking carefully, she came to a spot where there was a tuft of buffalo hair. Nestled in the hair there was a buffalo rock; this was the person who was singing.

 Buffalo Rock instructed Weasel-Woman to sleep away from the camp for four nights and to seek a vision. During the four nights she was given instructions about the ritual and songs of the iniskim. After she had returned from her vision experience, Weasel-Woman instructed a young unmarried man who had been chosen as the leader of a buffalo drive. She taught him a song that would lead the buffalo into the drive lane and over a cliff (cf. Grinnell 1962: 229):

Man says, "Woman, iniskim, man.
They are powerful."
Man says, "Those rocks, I move them around.
It is powerful."
Woman says, "Those rocks, I move them around.
It is powerful."

Good running of buffalo.
The driver is coming with them.
We have fallen them [over the cliff].
We are happy.
     (Wissler and Duvall 1908: 87)

In other versions of this tradition, women played a central role in the initial reception of the vision and were the first to learn the songs and ritual practices (Wissler and Duvall 1908: 87–88; Grinnell 1962: 125–26). In the case of the Weasel-Woman tradition, the power of the buffalo song was transferred to the young man who was to lead the drive, and at the same time Weasel-Woman transferred the bundle to her husband. In a Northern Blackfeet version, however, the woman who received power from the buffalo rock maintained control over the ritual. But the first time the ritual was performed, a mistake was made, and the buffalo bulls that had been driven into the corral broke out. Then the women performed a dance before the iniskim, and the next day buffalo cows came in great numbers to the camp. They did not break through the enclosure, and the people had plenty to eat (Wissler and Duvall 1908: 89).

Iniskims became very widespread among the Blackfeet and provided their owners power that was exercised both for their families and for the good of the people. Owners of these bundles kept them carefully enclosed in buffalo hair and wrapped in the skin of an unborn buffalo calf. The bundle was suspended from a tripod that was placed behind their tipi, and it was bathed in the smoke of a sweetgrass smudge at the beginning of each day and again in the evening before it became dark (Wissler 1912: 243).

Among the Crows, rocks also appeared as persons in vision experiences; in such contexts they revealed their gender and special powers and the taboos to be observed. Often they were observed to emit an odor that smelled like sweetgrass, and it was believed that if male and female rocks were left to themselves, they would reproduce (Wildschut 1960: 91; Lowie 1922: 385). The bundles with which rocks were associated had many functions, including healing, war making, and hunting. In the case of hunting bundles, the rocks were believed to have the power to draw the buffalo.

The general symbolic associations surrounding rocks could be traced to some of the Crow origin traditions. In one version of the creation tradition, for example, First Worker created both Old Man Coyote and Rockman. In this narrative, Rockman married Tobacco, and from this union descended all of the people on the earth (Wildschut 1960: 97). According to this view, Rock was one of the oldest beings on earth; it is not surprising, then, that the Crows accorded such power to the rocks they encountered in their dreams and waking visions.

Crow rock bundles that were focused on hunting might contain animal body parts, such as the hoofs of buffalo or deer; if the bundle was employed in trapping, then a beaver foot might be included. The rock bundles that were used in hunting were owned by men who were called upon to open them during the early spring and late fall. The ritual that was enacted during the opening of these bundles was known as the "singing of the cooked meat" (Wildschut 1960: 97).

These powerful rocks were known as well among the Hidatsas, Gros Ventres, and Arapahoes (Wissler 1912: 244–45; Pepper and Wilson 1908). But they were incorporated into ritual processes that, because of their different origin traditions, had meanings that were peculiar to each group (see, for example, Pepper and Wilson 1908). Buffalo rocks were also incorporated into ritual processes associated with larger and more complex bundles. Among the Blackfeet, one of these larger ritual objects was the beaver bundle, which, according to some of its origin traditions, was transferred after a kinship relation was established between this animal and the people.

The kinship relation arose as a consequence of a sexual encounter between Beaver and a Blackfoot woman who was the wife of a good hunter. After a time a young beaver child was born to the woman, but rather than becoming angry, the husband came to have great affection for the young child. Seeing this, Beaver transferred to the man a ritual and songs and showed him all of the items that should be gathered to form the beaver bundle (Wissler and Duvall 1908: 75–76; cf. Grinnell 1962: 117–24; McClintock 1968: 103–12).

When this bundle was described by anthropologists and other observers in the late nineteenth and early twentieth centuries, it had evolved into the largest of such ritual objects among the Blackfeet. During the course of this development, a very complex ritual process containing several hundred songs as well as intricate dances had emerged. In addition to a pipe, sticks to mark the months of the year, rattles, body paints, and sweetgrass, the primary beaver bundle contained the body parts and skins of most of the animals in the Blackfoot environment: buffalo ribs, tails, and hoofs and the skins of beavers, muskrats, weasels, gophers, badgers, prairie dogs, antelopes, deer, mountain goats, wildcats, loons, blackbirds, ravens, woodpeckers, sparrows, crows, and ducks. A number of buffalo rocks were wrapped in buffalo hair and enclosed, along with the other items, in an elk skin that had been covered with red earth paint (Wissler 1912: 169).[5]

This large and impressive bundle was owned by one individual who, by virtue of this ownership, had a number of ritual responsibilities and had to abide by a long list of taboos. The responsibilities of the bundle fell also on the owner's wife, since she assisted in the care of the bundle and participated in its ritual processes. For example, "the owner's wife (the head wife, if more than one) takes care of the bundle and makes the smudge, morning, noon, and night. In the ceremony she leads the women in the evolutions and songs. *Her presence is necessary throughout*" (Wissler 1912: 172, my emphasis). There were several of these bundles among the three divisions of the Blackfeet, and, though they were understood to possess similar powers, they did not have identical contents. Furthermore, they could be transferred from one individual to another. These transfers were not as frequent as was the case for other bundles, however, because of the complexity of the ritual and because so much property was exchanged during the process. Clearly, ownership of this bundle carried with it significant social status as well as special responsibilities.

In addition to keeping track of time and predicting the weather, beaver bundle owners were called upon to open their bundles during the time when the Blackfeet planted and harvested tobacco; during the Sun Dance, since the Natoas or Sun Dance bundle was associated with the beaver bundle; and before buffalo drives when the buffalo were far away and needed to be drawn near the camps. The multiple functions of this bundle suggested that it had become interrelated with several ritual complexes during the course of its development.

When the people were facing hunger or the buffalo were far away, the beaver bundle owner conducted an animal-calling ritual (Wissler 1912: 204–9). A number of former owners and old men gathered in the owner's tipi to sing buffalo-calling songs and to participate in the ritual process. After sweetgrass was burned, the men gathered began to sing a buffalo song.

> Old Woman, she has come in with happiness.
> Old Man, he has come in with gladness.
> Man, he has come in with happiness.
> Buffalo, them I have taken.
> It is powerful.
> > (Wissler 1912: 205)

This song evoked the presence of Napi and his wife, Old Woman, and, in some versions, Sun and his wife, Moon. As the singing continued, some of the men who were seated before a rawhide image of a buffalo took the rattles contained in the bundle and while handling them sang a powerful raven song.

> That above, it is the raven's medicine.
> The wind, it is the raven's medicine.
> The raven, he is looking for buffalo.
> He has found them, he has taken them.
> Buffalo, them I have taken.
> > (Wissler 1912: 206)

Following a number of raven songs, the beaver bundle owner and his wife engaged in movements that imitated the buffalo. They bellowed, butted heads, and threw dust on themselves. Then they danced together with the hoofs and tail, making the movements and sounds of the buffalo. Their dance continued until they had circled the fire at the center of the tipi eight times. After this dance, the pipe contained in the bundle was lit, and smoke was offered to the Sun, the Moon, and the Wind. All who were present made gestures toward the bundle owner and his wife that symbolized receiving the gift of buffalo, saying, "Our hopes are that we shall all be made happy in the morning with plenty of meat" (Wissler 1912: 207).

Beaver bundle owners often participated in additional activities during times when the animals were being driven into the corrals or over cliffs. At other times, the beaver bundle owner might be called upon to perform animal-calling rituals with the buffalo rocks in his bundle. These bundle owners were sometimes asked to transfer some of the buffalo songs to others so that they might call the buffalo. Among the Blackfeet, this transfer took place between the beaver bundle owners and the owners of buffalo painted tipis (Wissler 1912: 231).[6] Two of these tipis featured striking images of Yellow and Black Buffalo. The Yellow Buffalo painted tipi had a buffalo cow painted across the back and a bull painted across the front; the life lines that ran the entire length of each animal were painted red and green. The animals on the Black Buffalo painted tipi were painted black against a white background; star symbolism was also prominent on this tipi (Grinnell 1901: 660–61).

The association of these buffalo tipis with the beaver bundle appeared in an origin tradition in which two young men received the tipis from underwater powers. They returned to their people and found them to be in a desperate condition; many were without food, and some were near starvation. The young men called upon the beaver bundle owners and told them to bring their buffalo rocks and their rattles. "They asked the beaver men to give them songs. . . . In payment, the beaver men received the buffalo hoofs. Long afterwards the woman who found the buffalo rock gave the tipi owners some of her songs for charming the buffalo and when the people want the buffalo to come near they call on the tipi owners to help charm them" (Wissler 1912: 231). At least in some versions of the oral tradition, then, the iniskim, the beaver bundle, and the buffalo painted tipis were associated; the rituals and songs used in one context could also be used in ritual contexts that focused on calling the buffalo. This example also illustrates the creative reinterpretation of both oral traditions and ritual processes.

The meanings that infused these bundles were especially clear when the buffalo tipis were transferred from one person to another (Wissler 1912: 233–34). The transfer ritual, which contained a very rich and textured symbolism, opened with a sweat lodge. Buffalo rocks were placed on top of the sweat lodge, and while the people were inside the lodge, buffalo and tipi songs were sung. The hole in which the heated rocks were placed was shaped in the form of a triangle, said to represent the heart of a buffalo. The owner of the tipi and his wife, along with the man and wife who were the purchasers, were the main participants in the ritual. The purchasers and sellers exchanged clothes, and the purchasers were painted yellow with white crosses on various parts of their bodies; after the transfer had occurred, their faces were painted red with white crosses. Then the four participants danced, making buffalo movements and sounds. After this dance was over, the transfer was complete (Wissler 1912: 232–34).

The beaver bundles, rock bundles, and painted tipis insured that the Blackfoot relation to the buffalo would be one that sustained the people and guarded them against starvation. Descriptions of Blackfoot hunting techniques as well as their highly developed knowledge of animal behavior showed that they were quite sophisticated hunters of buffalo and other game animals in their environment (Wissler 1910: 33–42). Skill alone, however, was insufficient, and any mature member of Blackfoot society would have considered it foolish to expect to have success in hunting without appealing to powers that transcended their considerable hunting skills. These powers, which could be released again and again through ritual processes, were embodied in the bundles, which were, to the Blackfeet, living entities. Power to call buffalo was combined with the knowledge and skill required to hunt and kill these animals; in this sense, religious meanings infused economic activities and rendered them both culturally significant and efficacious.

The Sweet Medicine traditions among the Cheyennes analyzed in the last chapter provide another example of a bundle that had great significance for hunting. This bundle contained the arrows received by Sweet Medicine during his sojourn in the mountain. Unlike the transfers so characteristic of the Blackfeet, the arrow bundle was kept by a single individual who was qualified by his virtuous behavior and ritual experience. The arrow keeper's body was scarified in a manner that would signal to the people his special role and relation to transcendent powers. The cardinal directions were inscribed upon his skin in the form of four scars that formed after strips of flesh were removed from each of his arms, shoulders, and thighs as well as his back and loins. Strips of flesh were also removed from the outside of each arm, beginning at the wrists; these strips extended to the shoulders and down the chest until they met at the sternum. At the point where the scars met, a round piece of flesh, symbolizing the sun, was removed; just above this sun symbol, a crescent-shaped piece of flesh, symbolizing the moon, was also removed (Grinnell 1910: 544–45).

When the arrow keeper became too old to perform his role, another qualified person would have to be found; but at any point in time, the Cheyenne people could see this person and would know that his special rituals kept them safe from their enemies as well as supplied with an abundance of food. This assurance came from the belief that two of the arrows gave the Cheyennes power during war, and two others that were buffalo arrows gave them power over the buffalo. The two buffalo arrows in the bundle enabled the people to kill as many of these animals as they needed. During a hunt, the arrow keeper pointed two buffalo arrows toward the herd, and as long as he maintained this position, the people could approach the buffalo freely. Each animal that was killed through the power of the arrow bundle was butchered in a special manner. The people took all of the meat but the head, which was left attached to the backbone and tail (Dorsey 1905a: 2). Ritual butchering implied not only that the animals would take offense if done otherwise but also that the animals would not be renewed if butchering was done improperly.

Another Cheyenne ritual process that focused specifically on hunting was related by some interpreters to the Yellow-Haired Woman tradition analyzed in the last chapter (Schlesier 1987: 76–78). This was an animal dance of great complexity known as the Massaum (for a fuller description, see Grinnell 1972, 2: 285–336). Before the destruction of the buffalo, this ritual was held annually during the summer, perhaps in the vicinity of Bear Butte, where Sweet Medicine received the arrow bundle. A central figure in the ritual was a woman who represented Yellow-Haired Woman and assumed her power to call the animals. Proper enactment of the Massaum ritual would ensure that during the hunting season that followed the animals would be drawn into the Cheyenne corrals.

The symbolism surrounding the arrangement of the Cheyenne encampment and the participation of a vast number of animal impersonators in the enactment were important aspects of the ritual.[7] The Cheyenne camp was arranged in a circle with the end facing Bear Butte left open. Inside the larger camp circle was a smaller circle of lodges that represented all of the game animals that the Cheyennes hunted on the Northern Plains. These lodges recalled the underground place from which Yellow-Haired Woman's father, Coyote-Man, had released the animals. At the open end of the two circles, drive lines were constructed, and a drive lane extended toward the center of the circle. At the end of the drive lane was an animal corral behind which stood the Massaum lodge; it was within this lodge that Yellow-Haired Woman and the other ritual participants were dressed and painted.

The Massaum ritual lasted five days, and on the last day all of the represented animals poured out of their dens. Yellow-Haired Woman stood in the corral, raised a pipe, and began to call the animals. They circled around the camp in a clockwise direction until they finally entered the drive lane. When the animals were in the corral, they were ritually hunted and killed by men who represented the Thunder spirits. At the end of this hunt, the Massaum was concluded, and the people moved off to their fall hunting territories. Hunting activities during the remainder of the year were infused with the power released by Yellow-Haired Woman as mistress of the animals. When combined with the buffalo arrows given by Sweet Medicine, Cheyenne hunters believed that the animals would come to their corrals and once again give themselves to the people.

Among the village societies, the Pawnees had complex ritual processes that surrounded the communal buffalo hunts that were conducted in the summer and winter.[8] Hunting rituals among the Pawnees were interrelated with a yearly cycle that began when the first signs of spring signaled the renewal of the earth (Murie 1984: 31). Like the Mandans and Hidatsas, the Pawnees lived in earth lodges and depended upon both agriculture and hunting. After their gardens were planted and the plants had begun to grow, the people left their villages for a summer buffalo hunt.

Among the Pawnees the social organization required to coordinate a hunt, including people from several villages, featured not only men who belonged to one of the societies to maintain order but also the powers associated with one of the village bundles.[9] The bundle was placed in a tipi erected in the center of the hunting encampment, and this tipi became the gathering place for the various village chiefs (Murie 1984: 98). During the time of the summer hunt, successive surrounds and kills were made until sufficient meat had been accumulated; at that point, the people returned to their respective villages.

During the communal hunts, there were two persons who had prominent roles. One of these men had shelled and distributed the sacred corn during the year, and the other had provided a new robe for covering the bundle that contained Mother Corn. The corn sheller remained in the chief's tipi while the other man went out among the hunters where he made "a smoke offering; then sitting erect, he recounts the fact that he gave the robe for Mother Corn and that she is now watching over the people to make this hunt very successful" (Murie 1984: 99).

Ritual processes that would be enacted during the remainder of the year required sacrifices of both meat and corn, and the summer hunt was an occasion to gather a sufficient quantity of meat to be set aside for such purposes. The man who had given the robe for Mother Corn was also required to offer a whole buffalo carcass to the bundle located in the chief's tipi at the center of the camp. In addition, other hunters might decide to identify a particular animal as holy, and after it had been butchered in a ritual manner, it was offered to one of the bundle priests (Murie 1984: 88). A number of other rituals might be enacted during the summer hunt that required that buffalo meat be offered to major bundles.

Winter hunts were also under the direction of a particular bundle. When the winter buffalo were scarce and the rituals associated with the bundle were inadequate to bring the animals near the camp, a special ritual was required in which Mother Corn was transferred from the bundle in charge of the hunt into the Evening Star bundle. The belief was that this act would allow the superior powers of the Evening Star bundle to be merged with the powers of the bundle in charge of the hunt. During the transfer ritual, buffalo songs were sung, and calf shoulder blades taken from the Evening Star bundle were hung in each of the four directions. One of these shoulder blades was burned during each of the four days involved in the transfer ritual (Murie 1984: 113).[10]

If the merging of the bundle powers brought buffalo, then the hunt was conducted in a special manner. The body parts that remained after butchering each animal were left in a pile rather than being distributed randomly, and the rib meat was brought to the lodge where the ritual had occurred. If a yellow calf was in the herd, this animal was killed, and its skin would become the new covering for the Evening Star bundle. The Pawnees believed that "when a yellow calf is found in winter, it leads the herd of cows; hence, if its power can be put into the bundle the people will surely have meat, for where the bundle is, the buffalo will come" (Murie 1984: 114).

In addition to these complex ritual processes, the Pawnees enacted a dance around twelve buffalo skulls that had been arranged in a semicircle. This animal dance was performed as late as 1872, before the Pawnees left for their annual summer hunt. In addition to the dancing, which lasted for three days, the leaders of the ritual prayed over the bows and arrows, as well as the other equipment used in the hunt, saying, "We are poor—Take pity on us—Send us plenty of buffalo, plenty of fat cows . . . help the people—send us plenty of meat so that we may be strong, and our bodies may increase and our flesh grow hard" (Grinnell 1961: 272). After these prayers were finished, the hunting equipment was placed within the semicircle formed by the buffalo skulls, and the dancing began.

The Mandans and Hidatsas also had several important buffalo-calling rituals that were associated with bundles. Because they had such long residence on the Missouri River and lived in relatively close proximity, and because of the pressure put upon their respective cultures by disease and warfare, they came to share some of these ritual processes; usually, however, the rituals were associated with oral traditions that incorporated them in a manner that gave their enactment a distinctive Mandan or Hidatsa flavor. Some of these rituals were also identified with similar origin traditions.

When they were recorded in the early decades of the twentieth century, these rituals and oral traditions may have been more systematic, because of the creative activities of native interpreters, than they were in earlier times. Even though systematization may have occurred, the rituals still provided a picture of earlier cultural practices, some of which were quite old. Among the Mandans and Hidatsas, these rituals generally followed the seasonal calendar and were enacted during specific times of the year.

By the time the buffalo had disappeared in the nineteenth century, the Hidatsa Earthnaming Bundle ritual had achieved dominance in relation to other animal-calling rituals; for this reason, the owner of this bundle occupied a very high status in the ritual life of the community (Bowers 1965: 437). For the Hidatsas, the Earthnaming Bundle also defined their hunting territory, which was bounded by specific buttes where powerful animal spirits, including the buffalo, lived; these spirits were under the leadership of a large owl who lived in the Killdeer Mountains. A periodic ritual was held in which all of the animal spirits, under the leadership of Owl, would participate.

Origin traditions associated with the Earthnaming Bundle attributed it to Raven Necklace, a young Assiniboine who had been captured and adopted by the Hidatsas. Because Raven Necklace did not push over a dead snag that was the home of Owl and his children, he received powerful information that was of benefit to the people. "This valley is known as Owl valley," the great bird said. "You can make a buffalo corral here" (Bowers 1965: 434). The corral was constructed, and the people had a very successful hunt. Their success was attributed to a bundle that had been transferred from Owl to Raven Necklace. The bundle, which contained buffalo-hide rattles, owl body parts, a buffalo skull, sage, and body paints, became central to a powerful animal-calling ritual among the Hidatsas.

Clearly, Northern Plains hunters believed that animal body parts, which were almost universally present in their bundles, had a causal connection to the behavior of living animals. It is not often clear what this connection was, but some of the traditions that have been covered suggested that dancing or ritual enactments involving animal body parts invoked the power of particular animal masters or animal spirits who could withhold or release the buffalo. While all bundles contained animal or bird body parts, there were those among the Mandans and Hidatsas that contained buffalo neckbones.

There is archaeological evidence that buffalo neckbones were buried very near, if not simultaneously with, humans (Bowers 1965: 463–64). This practice suggested that these bones may have been associated with personal hunting bundles that were buried along with their owner. Maximilian, who spent the winter of 1833–34 among the Mandans and Hidatsas, observed that the neckbones were preserved "with a view to prevent the buffalo herds from removing to too great a distance from them. At times they perform the following ceremony with these bones: they take a potsherd with live coals, throw sweet-smelling grass upon it, and fumigate the bones with the smoke" (1906: 375). Given what was said above, such activities were probably associated with the enactment of rituals that centered on bundles containing buffalo neckbones.

The Crows, who were Hidatsa kin, also had bundles that included buffalo body parts. One of these bundles arose as a consequence of a dream endured by a Crow named Long-Three-Year-Old-Buffalo (Wildschut 1960: 139–40). His sister had been killed, and during his time of mourning he went to the Crazy Mountains to seek a vision. In his vision, Long-Three-Year-Old-Buffalo saw a deer, but when he started to shoot it, it became a buffalo. He shot the buffalo, and although blood gushed from the wound, the animal disappeared, leaving behind only a small spot of buffalo grease and a stunted horn.

The next night Long-Three-Year-Old-Buffalo had another dream in which a buffalo gave him a ritual and a bundle containing three horns; one horn was for hunting, while the other two were for healing. The horn that was to be used for hunting required that it be ritually smudged and smeared with buffalo grease. While sleeping with this horn, Long-Three-Year-Old-Buffalo was shown where the buffalo and other game could be found. If this ritual practice failed, then he was to hang the horn around his neck, and its power would lead him to the place where buffalo herds were plentiful. In addition to the horns, which were painted red, the bundle contained two rattles, one of which had a buffalo tail attached to it. All of these objects were placed in a cylindrical rawhide case that had been painted with red, yellow, and blue geometric designs.

Another Hidatsa bundle, called Imitating Buffalo, was grounded in an origin tradition referred to in chapter 2. In this tradition, after First Creator and

Lone Man had formed the land on either side of the Missouri River, they encountered male buffalo on the earth. At a later time another figure, Village-Old-Woman, created female buffalo as well as other female animals to dwell on the earth with the male animals. After male and female animals were created, oral traditions told of a male predecessor named Blood Man and a female predecessor named Buffalo Woman. Blood Man, a master of the animals figure, and Buffalo Woman, a buffalo cow transformed into a Hidatsa woman, assisted the people in calling the buffalo and, in the distant past, saved them from starvation (Bowers 1965: 438). In this case, as in many others, buffalo established kinship with the people that made possible access to these animals for food.

The ritual associated with the bundle was traditionally held during winter. It focused on calling the buffalo that were associated with that season to come near the Hidatsa villages. Like many other rituals, Imitating Buffalo lasted four days; the major participants included a man representing Blood Man and a woman representing Buffalo Woman. The dances associated with this bundle were enacted by the major participants as well as by postmenopausal women who were members of the Holy Woman's Society and men who belonged to the Black Mouth Society, a group that enforced order in the villages (Bowers 1965: 442–46). At the symbolic level, imitating buffalo evoked the power associated with Blood Man and Buffalo Woman, and this power was believed to be efficacious in bringing animals near the villages.

Practices derived from a broader ritual complex surrounding Mandan eagle trapping had importance for successful corralling of the buffalo. Such practices, also associated with eagle trapping, were present among the Hidatsas as well (Bowers 1965: 446–51). The Mandans believed that a bundle associated with eagle trapping originated in the distant past when a man named Black Wolf who was near starvation was saved by a group of small black bears. These bears transferred to Black Wolf the songs and ritual knowledge associated with the bundle; the powerful beings who contributed to this bundle included "Old Black Bear, Coyote, Snake, Buffalo, Young Eagle, and Little Black Bear" (Bowers 1950: 216). Included in this bundle was a snare that was used to bring the buffalo into the corrals. During the time of the hunt, the owner of an eagle-trapping bundle would stand "on a high hill in full view of the activities and out of the path of the buffaloes. . . . The man with the snare made movements as though snaring the animals, singing the Snare song and praying to the Black Bears to bring the buffaloes into the corral" (Bowers 1965: 448; see also 1950: 255).

The use of snare imagery was very widespread, not only on the Northern Plains but also among other North American hunters. For example, the Wahpeton Dakotas, located in present-day Manitoba, had a tradition that featured Spider and involved the construction of a snarelike enclosure (Wallis 1923: 65–66). After the people appealed to Spider for assistance, this being called all of the game animals into a forest. When the animals arrived he wove a web around the forest, and the people were able to kill all of them. Clearly this tradition represented Spider as trickster, since he called the animals for the ostensible purpose of having an important meeting. There were other possible associations as well, since Spider could also be interpreted as an animal master.

Women, Sexuality, and Ritual Process

Other hunting rituals based on bundles included the participation of women in a different manner. In these rituals, hunting power was believed to be transferred through sexual intercourse (see Peters 1995: chap. 11; Kehoe 1970). Two of these, the Snow Owl and the Red Stick, were enacted by the Mandans during the winter months. While both of these bundles were employed for other purposes, their buffalo-calling powers were of central importance to the people's well-being. The Snow Owl bundle contained materials for the construction of arrows, since it was also associated with arrow-making rituals, which, along with pottery making, were activities infused with transcendent significance. Also included were a grapevine, a fawn skin, two owl feet, body paints, an owl wing feather, sage, a bow and lance, a buffalo robe, magpie feathers, and a pipe (Bowers 1950: 285).

The oral tradition associated with the origin of the ritual included the figure of Black Wolf as well as the Buffalo Woman who lived in Dog Den Butte. The ritual was enacted in an earth lodge that symbolized Dog Den Butte and was held during four successive winter nights. The participants included the bundle owner and his wives, a woman who represented Buffalo Woman, and a man who represented Buffalo Woman's brothers. The ritual was enacted in response to the request of a young man who had powerful buffalo dreams. The central act that transferred buffalo power and insured success in the winter hunt had been required by Buffalo Woman: "In the future, when any Indian thinks of me, he must make offerings to me and give his wife to the one who is the head of this medicine" (Bowers 1950: 283).

In the origin tradition, Buffalo Woman had danced, naked except for a buffalo robe and a small turtle shell that covered her genitals, and the woman who represented her in the Snow Owl ritual did the same. She was joined by a number of older, experienced hunters who represented the buffalo bulls. In the audience were a number of clan brothers who had brought their wives to "walk with the buffalo." As each dance came to a close, one of these young women would approach an older man chosen by her husband and ask that he "walk" (have sexual intercourse) with her. If the older man agreed, then the people believed that his buffalo power would be transferred, through sexual intercourse, to the young woman and then, through sexual intercourse with her husband, to her family. At the end of the ritual, the central participants entered a sweat lodge and, after a meal, reentered the world of everyday life (Bowers 1950: 284–85).

Among the Hidatsas, the Red Stick ritual was based on an origin tradition that featured a sexual encounter between Buffalo Woman and Sun (Bowers 1965: 453), while the Mandan origin tradition was associated with Corn Silk. In this tradition, Corn Silk had brought a little girl, who turned out to be a cannibal, to the Mandan village (Bowers 1950: 319–23). After this girl had eaten a number of people, a young man went out to fast and pray, hoping to find out what had been happening to his people. While he was isolated on a hill, the young man saw twelve buffalo bulls coming toward him through the snow. Each of them carried a red stick to which were attached buffalo body parts. They revealed to the young man that the girl was a cannibal and transferred to him knowledge of the Red Stick ritual; the bundle thus established contained twelve red sticks to which were attached buffalo hoofs and a buffalo robe that symbolized the young girl.

Like the Snow Owl, this ritual involved young men offering their wives to older hunters who, in the dance, represented the buffalo bulls. Before sexual intercourse took place, however, the young women formed a line facing the twelve red sticks, which had been placed end to end on the floor of the lodge. Each woman removed her buffalo robe, squatted on her heels, and walked astraddle the red stick line until she had reached the end. This dramatic representation of intercourse with the buffalo was followed by actual intercourse with the older men, who had themselves become, through the ritual, buffalo bulls. As they left the lodge, often the "grandfather" could be heard bellowing like a buffalo bull (Bowers 1950: 317–18).

Among the Arikaras there was a hunting bundle that also featured potent fertility symbolism in some of its origin traditions (Howard 1974). Some of these traditions were introduced in the last chapter, but there was an additional tradition that followed the familiar pattern of intercourse with the buffalo; as a consequence, the people received a buffalo ritual and bundle as well as a buffalo game (Dorsey 1904a: 94–101). This tradition had as one of its central characters a young man, a superb hunter, who was known among the people as Man-Who-Kills-Game-Easily.

While out hunting this young man had a vision in which he saw two buffalo bulls playing a game with a buffalo cow. In language that clearly suggested sexual intercourse, each of the bulls said of the cow, "I will ring her" (Dorsey 1904a: 94). As they ran toward her, they became sticks and she became a ring. After Man-Who-Kills-Game-Easily awoke, he saw a buffalo cow lying on the ground. After he had sexual intercourse with the cow, the animal disappeared, and the young man saw a ring, identical to the one in his vision, lying on the ground. He cut sticks (buffalo bulls) to go with the ring (the buffalo cow's vagina) and returned to his village. He became very skilled in playing the game, catching the ring on the stick every time he played.

After a number of adventures, the young man encountered the buffalo cow with whom he had had intercourse and learned that he had a buffalo-son. As the buffalo cow and calf returned to their people, Man-Who-Kills-Game-Easily followed, and when they got to the buffalo village he presented the buffalo bulls with gifts of eagle feathers. But because he ran out of feathers, the bulls who did not receive presents became angry and threatened to kill him. After a number of trials, the young man's powers were established, and the buffalo people decided to give themselves to the people for food. The leader of the buffalo also presented the young man with a special gift: "This day I give you sticks to play with. The two sticks are people. The ring is a kind of people—the Buffalo" (Dorsey 1904a: 101). The buffalo calf then transferred to the people the ritual and its associated bundle.

This Arikara hunting bundle was used to call the buffalo and was central to the ritual of the Arikara Buffalo Society, which was composed of men who had buffalo power; their dances were focused on calling the buffalo near the villages. The stick and ring game, given by the buffalo, seems to have functioned in a multivalent symbolic context: the game represented the "ringing" of the animals, and, in this sense, it suggested the symbolism of a snare. The game also evoked memories of the kinship relations between the Arikaras and the buffalo people that were established when He-Who-Kills-Game-Easily had sexual relations with the buffalo cow.

A Lakota tradition that featured the hoop but lacked explicit sexual symbolism portrayed the people living east of the Missouri River in the northern part of the present state of Minnesota (Walker 1905).[11] The people were exhausted and hungry; given the circumstances, a young man decided to seek a vision and begin his fast. After two days the people in the camp saw a buffalo approach the hill where the young man was fasting. When he returned to the camp, the young man told the people that the buffalo had given him a bundle and that he had received important instructions that would be of benefit to the people. He told them to erect a tipi in the middle of the camp circle and to select four men to be his assistants. Then he entered a sweat house, and when he emerged he opened the bundle that had been given by the buffalo. It contained a pipe, the stem of which was painted red and the bowl of which was made of black stone.

The young man then instructed his assistants to gather four cherry sticks and an ash sapling. He took one of the cherry sticks and formed it into a hoop, which he held in the smoke from a sage smudge; he then painted it red. Then the young man said to the four men, "Now I shall roll the hoop. It will circle the tent. You are to watch the tracks made by it. You will see that it

animal rituals

leaves buffalo tracks, returns to me, and lies down . . . [and] the young man said that, on the fourth day from this time, there would be many buffalo." The buffalo came to the camp as he had predicted, and the people "had a great hunt. Buffalo were everywhere. They even ran through the camp, and were shot down at the doors of the tents. The people had meat in great abundance" (Walker 1905: 282). After that time, whenever the people were without food, the four young men would play the hoop game, and the buffalo would always appear.

An Arikara buffalo-calling ritual that may or may not be related to the Buffalo society employed a notched bone from a human forearm; a stick was drawn across the notch to make a rasping sound (Lowie 1915a: 675). The use of a human body part probably recalled the traditions that told of the time when buffalo hunted and killed humans for food. When this ritual was enacted, the participants danced in a manner that imitated the movements of the buffalo. If this dance was performed in connection with the Buffalo society bundle ritual, then clearly the people must have felt considerable confidence when they sent their young men out to drive animals into their corrals.

An important Mandan and Hidatsa hunting ritual that was controlled by women was enacted during the winter by the White Buffalo Cow Society. Along with the Goose Society, which focused upon agriculture, the White Buffalo Society was the highest of the women's age-graded societies.[12] The ritual was enacted among both the Mandans and the Hidatsas, and although they performed separate rituals, the probability was that it originated with the Mandans and was transferred to the Hidatsas (Bowers 1950: 325). The White Buffalo Cow society included women past the age of menopause, an interesting symbolic contrast to the two previous rituals, which featured transfers of power by means of sexual intercourse with younger women.

The tradition of origin, narrated by Scattercorn, attributed the rise of the society to the dream experience of an unnamed man (Bowers 1950: 325–26). In his dream, the man heard the voice of Buffalo, who told him that two young children would soon arrive at the village. These children were left at the village by a group of women who were, in reality, buffalo cows. The buffalo cows showed the people how to enact the ritual, and when they left, one of the buffalo-children remained behind and was raised by the people.

When the ritual was enacted, the members of the White Buffalo Cow society gathered in a lodge to dance. They wore buckskin dresses, a headband made of white buffalo hair, and the feathers of an eagle and a magpie; the leading woman wore a robe that had been taken from a white buffalo. A buffalo skull was placed on the floor of the lodge where the women danced, and a child who represented the buffalo child in the oral tradition participated in the ritual. An observer of this dance in the mid-1800s said of the dancing that it was "kept up vigorously night and day until buffaloes came" (Boller 1959: 222). On this particular occasion, the people were astonished at the size of the herds that soon appeared near their villages.

The Blackfeet also had a women's society called the Matoki that enacted a ritual that was probably associated with driving buffalo into a corral (Wissler 1913: 430–35). This ritual took place over a four-day period in a specially constructed enclosure. Four men served as singers for the society, and two men were chosen to perform various tasks associated with the ritual; all of the major participants, however, were women. During the course of the ritual, the women made the movements and sounds of buffalo cows. At the conclusion of the four days a buffalo drive occurred in which the women of the Matoki, who had ritually become buffalo cows, were moved into a drive lane. They were driven into the Matoki lodge, which had become a buffalo corral.[13]

Dances, Symbolic Representation, and Leadership

Although the ritual use of hunting bundles almost always involved symbolic movements and often dancing, there were dances associated with hunting that did not feature bundles of the sort discussed up to this point. The clothing worn in the dances, especially the animal masks, shared some of the social functions of bundles, however, and could be transferred or inherited. Among the Santees, one of the Siouan groups located east of the Missouri River, there was such a buffalo dance (Lowie 1913: 119–21).[14] The men who were qualified to perform this dance had buffalo dreams and, on the basis of these experiences, formed a dance association. They usually danced during summer hunts, wearing masks that had been made of hide taken from a buffalo's head with the horns left attached. This hide was stuffed and, when dry, retained the original shape of the living animal. The participants were painted with vermillion or daubed with mud, and when they danced they wore buffalo tails and made the movements of the animals that were being pursued in the hunt.

The use of buffalo masks was widespread, and among the Ojibwas, men who had buffalo dreams wore such headdresses while they danced; in this case, an equal number of women danced as well (Skinner 1914: 507). According to George Catlin, the masked dancers among the Iowas were motivated by the belief that "there is some invisible spirit presiding over their [the buffaloes'] peculiar destinies, and before they have any faith in their hunts for them, that spirit must needs be consulted in a song, and entertained with a dance" (cited by Murie 1914: 713). Among the Menominis, there was a buffalo dance led by a man who possessed a buffalo headdress; the participants in this dance were qualified by virtue of their powerful buffalo dreams (Skinner 1915b: 201–2).

Buffalo-calling rituals among Northern Plains peoples clearly developed over time and increased in complexity as rituals, dances, songs, and bundles were integrated into each respective culture. There were additional ritual processes associated with communal hunts that contributed to an understanding of the religious complexity that characterized Northern Plains societies. Among the Lakotas, for example, George Sword provided the basis for an account of a communal hunt that described ritual aspects that accompanied this important activity.

Before the planning process could get under way, a shaman sought a vision. The communication received in the vision determined the prospects for success on the hunt or, in some cases, would lead the people to conclude that no hunt should be undertaken at that time. If the vision was favorable, then the shaman would paint a buffalo skull red and attach to it a number of feathers and smaller bundles containing special materials that he had concluded would influence Tatanka, the spirit who controlled the outcome of the hunt. Then the chief and other important leaders met in council to offer a pipe "to the skull of the buffalo and the Spirit of the Buffalo was called upon to give aid in the chase and to intercede with Tatanka, that he might bring the buffalo in plenty and make their chase successful" (Walker 1982a: 76).

After it had been determined that a hunt would occur, the people were organized under the leadership of young men who had been given authority over the people during their movements toward the hunting territory. They oversaw the movements of the camp and enforced the rules that governed behavior of all during this crucial period. While the people were moving, shamans often sought additional visions, seeking thereby to gain further information concerning the outcome of the hunt. During this time, hunters would also play the hoop and pole game, which was believed to have influence over the buffalo.[15]

When the buffalo were located, a shaman would smoke while resting his pipe on a buffalo chip. The buffalo chip embodied the presence of Tatanka, and his power was invoked at this critical time. Other ritual acts sometimes accompanied the capture of animals. In these cases, a shaman might "explain to a captured one [animal] that this is his destiny, then decorate it as a mark of friendship, and, freeing it, bid it tell its kind what he said and did to it" (Walker 1917: 92). The shaman was also careful to see that none of the hunters violated any of the ritual taboos that surrounded the hunt: "A man might so offend the game animals that they will escape from the hunters, and if so a shaman should penalize the offending one by making taboo some portion of the offended animals" (Walker 1917: 92).

After the hunt had been successfully concluded, one of the buffalo carcasses was offered to Tatanka. In the rare instances when a white buffalo was killed, the carcass was left where it fell after having been skinned. The people believed that, in such times, "the spirit of the buffalo took up its abode there [in the carcass], pleased with the generosity of the people" (Walker 1982a: 93).[16] When the meat was being cut up, divided, and dried, a shaman sought an additional vision that often led to further ritual actions or gift giving on the part of the people. These rituals focused upon the repayment to the spirits who had presided over the hunt and were done by the people in a spirit of gratitude for the food they had received.

The Assiniboines also enacted interesting rituals during their spring hunt

(Lowie 1909: 52–55). Like many other Northern Plains nomads, the Assiniboines were divided during the winter into smaller hunting bands composed of members of several extended families. As the summer approached, the people looked forward to communal activities such as the Sun Dance and corporate hunting expeditions. In preparation for the communal hunts a man who had pledged to enact the Sun Dance held a feast, inviting all of the older and distinguished men to attend. They spent considerable time reciting their exploits in war and smoking a black pipe to which horse and human hair was attached. When this phase of the meeting was concluded, a chief took tobacco and divided it into four separate portions. Young men who were known to be brave volunteered to take the bundles of tobacco to other Assiniboine groups. When one of these young men arrived at a distant camp, he presented the tobacco to an assembled group that included the chief and other distinguished older men. If the tobacco was accepted and smoked, then the people of this band were committed to join the other Assiniboine groups in a communal hunt. After all four tobacco bundles had been accepted the different bands met and set off together to the place where a buffalo corral had been constructed.

The medicine person responsible for the hunting rituals set up a buffalo-calling pole at the center of the corral; to this pole were attached pieces of brightly colored cloth, tobacco, and the horn of a buffalo. At the corral this ritual director fasted while he sang, beat his drum, and sought powerful visions. The scouts that were searching for the animals carried with them a ball of buffalo hair, which provided them with additional power to locate the game. When the buffalo were found, the buffalo-hair ball was sent back to the shaman, and the animals were usually successfully driven into the corral.

Interpreting the Rituals

The animal rituals discussed in this chapter were grounded in complex symbolic networks mediated in the oral traditions of the various groups. Interpreting the meanings that constituted these symbolic networks has been only partially adequate, given the variety of interests and theoretical perspectives of the anthropologists and others who recorded them. For these reasons, the

animal rituals

meaning and purpose of the rituals are only partially visible, and in some instances the interpretations rendered may not simply be partial but may actually be in error. Even though there are such inevitable risks associated with the task, some themes seem evident in the material.

Northern Plains buffalo-hunting rituals were clearly aimed at practical results in the everyday world—the provision of food and other items necessary for human life. In this sense, the meaning of the symbolic networks enacted in the rituals was fundamentally performative. These rituals were characterized by body movements, paints, and scarification, as well as forms of dress such as masks. The rituals were also often focused on the manipulation of the pipes, animal body parts, and other materials that made up any accompanying bundles.

Furthermore, the symbolic networks were enacted in such fashion that a distinction does not seem to be drawn—except by some interpreters—between ritual actions and the desired outcome. That is, symbols did not *represent* realities to which they referred as, for example, animal dancers *represented* buffalo movements or, in another term used, "mimicked" the animals. Even though the use of such terms has been almost unavoidable, it appears that Northern Plains peoples believed that the ritual enactment embodied transcendent realities and made them manifest in the everyday world.

Because of the intrinsic connection between ritual enactment and transcendent realities, the complex animal rituals among Northern Plains groups produced the kind of double vision that we saw embodied in the Cree narrative about the young man who took a caribou wife and in the Eskimo narrative about the boy who went to live with the seals. In these traditions, discussed in the last chapter, hunting was experienced both from the perspective of the hunter and the animals that were hunted. While many of the hunting rituals and the oral traditions that were presented in this chapter and the last were not as explicit as these narratives, still this double perspective was often constituted and maintained.

Humans who received hunting power from animals, especially when kinship relationships were established, saw clearly that the buffalo-people had families, children, and a social structure comparable to the humans. In many of the narratives, both the human and the animal husband or wife had their own children. Once these relationships had been established, the human-animal child or the animal wife or husband mediated between the two peoples, the animal and the human. In these narratives, sexual encounters between humans and animals could at times have the purpose of control over animals; in other instances, erotic encounters led to a structure of mutual obligation because a family was constituted. The animals assumed kinship obligations to the humans and gave themselves to the people for food, and the people assumed reciprocal obligations to their animal kin. In some instances, erotic feelings and dreams were connected with hunting, killing, and consuming animal flesh.[17]

These rituals and their oral traditions also generated a powerful vision of the depth and complexity of human life. Humans were bound in dense webs of powerful relationships with human others as well as with a myriad of transcendent persons who often took the form of animals. The transcendent spirits who took the form of animals, as well as the animal spirits that were encountered in dreams and waking visions, were embodied in a manner that generated a transformative expectation in the experience of Northern Plains peoples. Humans appeared to be human, but then they became animals; these beings often continued to be transformed in a seemingly confusing sequence of narrative events that often included betrayals, contests, and power struggles. Likewise, animals who appeared in their animal form at one point took the form and language of the humans at another point. All of this occurred within the context of a struggle on the part of humans who, in order to live, must establish relationships with these powers, including animal spirits, in order to be successful in killing animals for food. The final mysteries of such fundamental needs and relationships were not completely solved by Northern Plains peoples. But they addressed these mysteries in their religions, they stretched toward them through vision and symbolic forms, and they sought to enact them in their ritual processes.

The theme of sexual encounters between human hunters and animals and the rituals that were generated as a consequence clearly had a relation to beliefs about the fertility and reproduction of the animals. Examples of these motifs were evident in the case of the Mandan Snow Owl and Red Stick rituals. Broader themes concerning the renewal of the animals were prominent in a class of rituals that have been alluded to but not yet completely analyzed. On the Northern Plains, these rituals were often referred to by the general term "Sun Dance," but upon closer examination it becomes clear that each society had its own particular understanding of the meaning of these ceremonies. The buffalo symbolism and the ritual processes that surrounded beliefs about the renewal of this animal are the subject of the next chapter.

renewing

5

the

animals

The meanings that infused hunter-animal relationships were evoked in the experience of Northern Plains peoples by the complex hunting rituals explored in the last chapter. These rituals, by nurturing the belief that animals would continue to give themselves for food, gave the people confidence that their lives would be sustained, and these beliefs were usually confirmed by successful hunts. While the rituals were specifically focused upon influencing the outcome of the hunt, they also embodied meanings associated with the wider symbolic networks discussed in earlier chapters. For example, memories concerning relationships between humans and animals established by legendary predecessors such as animal masters could have been a part of this experience, and in some cases these predecessors were represented in the hunting rituals.

More fundamentally, memories surrounding origin traditions deepened the context and rendered the interdependence of humans and animals even more complex. After all, powerful spirits in animal form were present at the beginning of the world and gave it shape through their actions. These meanings informed the direct and often anxious encounters with animals, encounters that issued in death, blood, and dismemberment on the one hand and the satisfaction of the hungers that are a part of every human condition on the other.

The shared cultural paradigms for understanding these encounters were embodied in the ritual processes we have studied up to this point. Northern Plains hunters also constructed ritual processes that were focused in particular ways on the renewal of the animals. Some of these rituals became known as Sun Dances, but this term does not comprehend the complexity and significance of these ceremonies since not all of them focused on a transcendent solar figure, and each was informed by particular cultural meanings. Despite their internal differences, these rituals were usually held annually and often occurred in connection with the gathering of the people for their summer hunt.

In many of these rituals, the renewal of the animals was symbolically associated with broader processes of world renewal. Among the Skidi Pawnees, for example, a Thunder ritual occurred in the spring; without this ritual, the people believed, the entire cycle of yearly renewal would be in jeopardy.[1] Furthermore, all of the Pawnee bundles, beginning with the Evening Star, had to be nourished by this ritual in order to renew their powers (Murie 1984: 43). This meant that the Thunder ritual was necessary in order for bundles, held by those "in charge" of the hunt, to achieve their fullest efficacy.

The Thunder ritual took place in an earth lodge and began with songs that reenacted the creation of the world. Four singers sat before an altar upon which had been placed, in addition to the bundle to be renewed, four ears of corn as well as the skins of an owl and a hawk. Behind the priests was a buffalo skull, and in front of the altar a path was marked, ending in a circle that was said to symbolize both the wisdom of the Pawnee predecessors and the inner core of human life. While these material features were important, it was the songs that were the most powerful: "The ritual is recited in the spring because it is conceived that just as the singing of the four gods in the west [Thunder, Lightning, Wind, and Cloud] originally helped in the creation of the earth, so the singing of the four priests in the ceremony at springtime will aid the powers to revivify the earth [including the animals], plants, water, and seeds and also replenish the powers in the bundle" (Murie 1984: 44). The symbols enacted in this ritual process were clearly connected with the transcendent powers that formed the earth and gave it life, so that through the ritual "the power of life is sent forth anew by the thunders every spring" (Murie 1984: 49).

In the Pawnee creation traditions discussed in chapter 2, Lightning was represented as the being who fertilized the earth with his powerful strikes. Some traditions indicated that Tirawa sent Lightning, a great giant, to make an assessment of the earth (Dorsey 1904b: 14). In the Thunder ritual there were songs to Lightning that told of this earth visit when he made contact with the various beings that he had struck with life. Among these beings were the buffalo, and the songs of the Thunder ritual celebrated the capacities infused by Lightning that enabled the humans to find these animals (Murie 1984: 51).

The ritual enacted the renewal of all of life, including the animals and plants so essential to the people's lives. This renewal was accomplished not simply because the ritual symbols "represented" the primal realities associated with Tirawa and the creation. Rather, the ritual work evoked the energies permeating the Pawnee world; without the ritual, these energies would begin to diminish. Such beliefs gave a pervasive sense of urgency to the ritual processes, for it was through these acts that the powers that energized the world at the beginning would reappear in each cycle of the seasons.

Among the Mandans, the renewal of the animals occurred as a consequence of rituals enacted as a part of the Okipa ceremony (see Bowers 1950: 111–63; Catlin 1967: 39–85). The Mandan villages had an open plaza for dances and other ritual processes. At the center of the plaza was a cedar post that symbolized the Mandan creator, Lone Man; in addition, there was a special lodge where the Okipa and other rituals were enacted. The Okipa lodge was "a symbol of Dog Den Butte where Hoita (the speckled eagle) imprisoned all living things" (Bowers 1950: 113).

The Okipa ritual was enacted at least yearly and evoked complex layers of meaning in the experience of the people. During the course of four days, the

renewing the animals

ritual recalled the creation of the earth and all living things as well as the history of the Mandans as a people. The narration of the creation traditions was not done by the uninitiated but was reserved for those who had inherited or purchased these rights. Furthermore, the ritual processes associated with the Okipa were conducted in an esoteric language that was not understood by the people at large (Bowers 1950: 111). Clearly, in the case of the Mandans, specialization and control of ritual knowledge were important features of the religious life.

Like the Pawnees, the Mandans had a successful dual economy based upon hunting and agriculture, and their rituals naturally included ceremonies that focused upon both corn and the buffalo. In addition to the Lone Man origin traditions discussed in chapter 2, the Mandans had traditions that told of Corn people who lived below the earth and who came to the surface far to the south, perhaps in the vicinity of the mouth of the Mississippi River on the Gulf of Mexico. Under the leadership of a culture hero named Good-Furred-Robe, these people migrated north along the Mississippi River until they came to the Missouri River. They continued north until they encountered the Buffalo people, who had been created by Lone Man on the Heart River. After meeting at the Heart River, the Corn and Buffalo people joined to form a culturally united group, but the animal rituals associated with the Okipa were believed to have originally been associated with the Buffalo people (Bowers 1950: 117).

The major participants in the ritual included a person who assumed the identity of Lone Man. Another person became Hoita, and a third assumed the identity of a Trickster-Clown. In addition, there were a number of persons who became animals and who danced before the people. There was also a company of young men who fasted and endured suffering in their pursuit of powerful visions. During the course of the ritual, these young men would have their chests and in some instances their back muscles pierced. Skewers were inserted into the cuts, and thongs were tied to the skewers; after the thongs were passed over one of the timbers forming the roof of the earth lodge, the young men were raised from the ground and left suspended until they lost consciousness. At this point, they were lowered to the ground, where they would endure the rich visions that were believed to accompany such experiences of intense suffering.

During the Okipa ritual, there were impressive animal dances, one of which was enacted by eight men who were dressed as buffalo bulls. They wore buffalo masks with sufficient skin attached to reach their waists, and their bodies were painted red, black, and white. When the buffalo bulls danced, they emerged from the Okipa lodge and oriented themselves toward the four directions around the cedar in the center of the plaza. Initially one pair of buffalo bulls was located at each cardinal direction, but during the dancing they separated: four dancers remained at the points of the cardinal directions while four moved to the points of the semicardinal directions.

Along with the persons dressed as various animals and birds, the bull dancers played a special role on the third day of the Okipa ritual. On this day there was a dance that released the animals from Dog Den Butte, making them available again for the people. All of the animals that had been imprisoned by Hoita came back on the third day, and they danced vigorously in the plaza and around the village. Mandans who watched from their positions on top of the surrounding earth lodges would have known traditions about Hoita and Lone Man, and their experience of this dance was enriched by deep familiarity with these narratives.

It was the interactions between the bull dancers and Mandan women that especially focused the energies necessary for renewing the buffalo. Before these primary interactions occurred, however, the Trickster-Clown had a role to play. This being was distinguished by a large wooden penis whose end was painted bright red. During the course of the dancing, he repeatedly sought to intimidate the women and to have intercourse with the buffalo bulls. His antics not only produced much laughter and joking among the people, but his foolishness was fully revealed when he tried to fertilize the male animals with his enormous penis. After his efforts, the Trickster-Clown was fatigued and was driven from the plaza by the women, one of whom captured his penis and brought it back to the village. This woman was given a fine dress and became the leader in a fertility ritual that renewed the buffalo (Catlin 1967: 69 71).

On the evening of the last night of the Okipa ritual, the woman who had defeated the Trickster-Clown, along with a number of young accomplices, gathered in the Okipa lodge along with the buffalo bulls. After a feast was held, the women began to dance before the buffalo bulls. In the course of dancing the women were transformed into female buffalo, then each of the buffalo women chose one of the bulls to have intercourse with. The fertilization and renewal of the buffalo continued until late in the evening, while the people not involved in the ritual remained quietly in their lodges. The sexual relationships between buffalo women and the buffalo bulls assured that the people would have plenty to eat during the coming year. When this ritual had ended, the major participants in the Okipa entered a sweat lodge; when they emerged there was a sense that one of the basic sources of the people's lives, the animals, had been renewed.

The cultural meanings that surrounded such activity focused upon the necessity to stimulate the fecundity of the buffalo by means of ritual processes that included sexual intercourse. Ritual intercourse between beings who had assumed an animal identity was assumed to produce the intended effects in the animal world. And in the case of most Northern Plains societies, such acts were given support by the many oral traditions concerning the beneficial consequences of human sexual encounters with animals. For example, the traditions concerning animal husbands and wives, explored in chapter 3, as well as the traditions that spoke of animal lovers were so widespread that they must have resonated in the experience of groups that practiced ritual sexual intercourse, giving a deep cultural legitimacy to these complex ceremonies.

On the Northern Plains, the rituals that became known as Sun Dances usually occurred during the summer buffalo hunt when the entire people gathered as a social unit. The summer encampment was also an occasion for extended social activities as well as ritual processes associated with the transfer or renewal of bundles. The Sun Dance was usually enacted in a structure built especially for this purpose. The general form on the Northern Plains was a circular structure surrounding a center pole. In addition, among many groups a special tipi was erected at the center of the camp circle; within this tipi, preparations for the Sun Dance took place. It was here that persons were instructed in the details of the ritual, their bodies were painted, and special forms of dress and other ritual objects were prepared.

The major participants in Northern Plains Sun Dances usually included a man and his wife, one of whom had pledged to sponsor the ritual. If a bundle transfer was involved, as it was in the case of the Blackfeet, then the bundle owner and his wife would also participate, and in some instances, all of those persons who had previously been Sun Dance pledgers had the right to participate in the preparatory aspects of the ritual. In addition, there were a number of individuals who had vowed to engage in intense suffering. Their chests were skewered, and the thongs that were tied to these skewers were attached to the center pole. Tethered in this fashion, these individuals would dance, pulling back against the thongs, until the flesh was torn. In this condition they often experienced powerful, life-shaping visions.

Among the Cheyennes, the Sun Dance was given to the people by Erect Horns, the Suhtai culture hero; the powerful themes of world renewal so evident in these traditions were discussed in chapter 3. These themes were also evident in the ritual processes that took place before the construction of the Sun Dance structure in a lodge known as the Lone-Tipi. This tipi was erected within the camp circle and had many symbolic associations, one of which—"hill from which buffalo came"—recalled the mountain from which Erect Horns brought forth the animals (Dorsey 1905b: 62). The ground within Lone-Tipi was cleared, exposing the barren earth; a border around the edge, where the participants would sit, was covered with sage and buffalo robes. Chief among these participants were the person who pledged the Sun Dance and his wife, who became identified with the woman who had accompanied Erect Horns on his journey.

Within the Lone-Tipi, a series of acts initiated world renewal. The person in charge of the ritual took the lodge-maker's thumb and traced a small, round earth on the barren ground within the Lone-Tipi. Later that day a second, slightly larger earth was formed with the palm of the lodge-maker's hand. Not only was this earth larger than the first, but it was made by rocking motions of the hand, motions that were identified with the wallowing of the buffalo; indeed, this second earth was linguistically identified as a buffalo wallow (Dorsey 1905b: 80). At this point in the ritual process, the buffalo were beginning to be renewed.

Two more larger earths were formed, indicating that revivifying powers were expanding. Then a fifth earth, also understood to be in the form of a buffalo wallow, was shaped in front of a buffalo skull that had been brought into the Lone-Tipi. This buffalo skull was painted red; alternating black and white lines were superimposed on the red; the eye sockets were filled with plugs of grass; and sun and moon symbols were painted on the jaws (Dorsey 1905b: 96–97). After the construction of the Sun Dance lodge, this buffalo skull occupied a central place at an altar that was constructed within the Sun Dance structure.

The altar was dug within the Sun Dance lodge, and the painted buffalo skull was placed at the back of the excavation. A semicircular mound of earth was formed around the skull. Into this semicircle were thrust sprigs of live foliage from trees and bushes, and a dry sand painting was done in the excavated space in front of the skull. This sand painting involved a dense color symbolism. Four solid lines—red, black, white, and yellow—were painted, and between these lines were dots that represented stars. The white line was the path of the lodge-maker and his wife, the red line was the path of the people (Cheyennes), the black line was the trail of the buffalo, and the yellow line was the path of the Sun. Clearly, for those who participated in the ritual, as well as for those who observed, this altar was a model of the world renewed; not only this, it was a symbolic representation that brought renewal into being.[2]

Among the Lakotas, the individuals who had decided to dance and suffer in the Sun Dance chose, from among those qualified, a shaman to serve as an instructor in the details of the ritual. As a part of this process, an altar was constructed in the dancers' lodge. All of the grass, weeds, and living things in the ground were removed by the shaman so that nothing would come into contact with the materials placed on the altar. After the altar had been prepared, a buffalo skull was painted with stripes of red paint; a similar stripe was painted on the candidate's forehead and on each side of his head. According to one interpretation, "The stripes across the forehead indicate that the Buffalo God has adopted the Candidate as a hunka, or relative by ceremony. The red stripes on the sides of the skull indicate that the Buffalo God will give especial protection to the Candidate" (Walker 1917: 69, 136).

The Sun Dance altar was larger than those constructed in the candidates' tipis and required a skull that had been decorated with offerings from women who had been through the buffalo ceremony.[3] After this skull was prepared and offerings were attached to its horns, it was addressed formally and told that the offerings symbolized the respect that the people had for the Buffalo God. Then the people feasted on a meal of dried or fresh buffalo tongues. This feast evoked multiple meanings, central among which was an appeal to the Buffalo God to renew the animals and provide the people with abundance (Walker 1917: 98).

When the candidates who were to dance and suffer entered the Sun Dance lodge, each carried the painted buffalo skull that had rested on the altar in his tipi. In one description, the altar in the Sun Dance lodge was dug in the shape of a crescent moon; all of the living material, plants as well as ground creatures, was removed. It was upon this bare ground within the moon-shaped altar that the candidates deposited their buffalo skulls (Dorsey 1894: 460). For the Lakotas, who believed that the locus of the animal's potency was in the head (Walker 1917: 98), enormous power had been concentrated in the altar. While this power radiated outward and affected all that occurred during the Sun Dance, a central assurance evoked by the powerful skulls was that the Buffalo God would provide for the renewal of the animals.

In addition to the Lakotas, Cheyennes, and Arapahoes, other groups as well had Sun Dance altars that featured buffalo skulls. Such structures were found among the Crows, Atsinas, Hidatsas, Assiniboines, Plains Crees, and Plains Ojibwas (Spier 1921: 466). While the Blackfeet had an altar within the Sun Dance lodge that was formed by clearing the ground, it apparently did not include a buffalo skull as a central ritual object. In most Northern Plains Sun Dances, however, buffalo skulls clearly played a central role. They presided over the ritual from their position behind an altar, suggesting that their renewing power proceeded from this place and would affect the people's lives during the coming year. In all of these cases, the belief that the animals would be renewed and would come to the people for food was deepened, and the confidence that life would flourish was given fundamental support.

There were some groups that gathered buffalo tongues, which were consumed either before or during the Sun Dance. The Lakotas, Atsinas, Blackfeet, and Crows were among those Northern Plains groups that had such a practice (Spier 1921: 463–64). For the Blackfeet, the meanings that surrounded the consumption of buffalo tongues were related, at least on the surface, to demonstrations of sexual purity, focusing particularly upon women. Although it is far from clear, some of the meanings that surrounded such ceremonies could also have to do with the identification of the people with the buffalo. The ingestion of this particularly prized body part by those gathered at the summer camp was certainly a symbolic act that reinforced their identity as a people. Furthermore, when the Blackfeet boiled the tongues, songs were directed to transcendent beings: Sun, Moon, Morning Star, and Buffalo. A few tongues were also painted and divided into small bits, and after a number of prayers, these pieces were buried in the ground (Wissler 1918: 237–38). Such ritual activities could certainly be viewed as pertaining to the renewal of the buffalo.

In addition to the hunt to obtain tongues, there was another hunt that was also conducted in a ritual manner. This hunt, which was to secure a buffalo hide for use in the Sun Dance, occurred among the Crows, Blackfeet, Atsinas, Arapahoes, and Arikaras. In some instances, such as the Blackfeet, the animal had to be killed with a single shot. In other cases the hunters followed prescribed rules, and the results of the hunt were often celebrated by additional ritual acts (Spier 1921: 464–65). The buffalo hide that was obtained as a consequence of the special hunt was often formed into the shape of a living animal and was hung on the center pole of the Sun Dance lodge.[4]

Rather than using the hide to form a complete animal image, the Blackfeet and the Atsinas cut thongs for lashing the timbers of the Sun Dance lodge together and for tying other materials to the center pole. Among the Blackfeet, cutting the thongs was embedded in a ritual process that was transferred from one individual to another. Persons who bought the right to cut the thongs were required to transfer property, often including a horse, to the individual who transmitted the ritual knowledge. Even though there was apparently no ritualized hunt associated with acquiring the buffalo hide that was used for the thongs, it seems consistent with the Blackfeet understanding to view the thongs as a symbolic distribution of the buffalo throughout the Sun's lodge. These meanings were condensed in a buffalo tail that hung from a thong from the top of the center pole. So the lodge may have evoked multiple symbolic meanings: as the Sun's lodge, as the cosmos or world, and as the buffalo. If this was true, then the renewing energies released by the ritual would involve, in addition to the personal and the social, the animal world as well.

The Arikaras and Hidatsas tied a buffalo skull to the center pole of their ritual structures. This skull was still attached to a strip of skin that ran along the animal's back. This strip of skin included the tail, and when it was fixed in place in the Sun Dance lodge it powerfully symbolized the renewed animal. These themes are quite explicit in rituals enacted with the skull placed at the altar in the Arapaho Sun Dance. These ritual processes took place during the time when the major participants were still involved in activities prior to the beginning of the Sun Dance proper. After a ceremonial hunt, the hide that was secured was taken into the preparatory tipi. After the front half of the robe was painted red and the back half black, it was placed carefully upon the decorated buffalo skull, the front of the hide touching the skull. As a consequence, "the buffalo skull and robe now constituted a living animal— Young-Bull. With the ceremonial killing of the buffalo, the life-element is transferred to the hide; this life-element is renewed or revivified as the hide is passed over the incense. With the placing of the robe over the skull . . . the process of forming an animate being is regarded as complete" (Dorsey 1903: 71). This synecdochical structure, in which a body part (or parts) comes to represent the whole animal, was a feature found not only in Northern Plains Sun Dances; this motif also pervaded the hunting rituals discussed in the previous chapter. The ritual significance of animal body parts was understood in the light of the oral traditions, which seems to suggest that bones and body parts embodied the power, the "personality," and the life force or "soul" of the animals with which they were associated.

Given these cultural meanings, rituals that institutionalized moral requirements concerning the treatment of animal bodies and body parts take on additional significance. For example, ritual prohibitions concerning the treatment of animal bodies were based upon beliefs that either the animal masters or the individual animals that were killed were present in spirit form. Given this perspective, the world of Northern Plains hunters was constituted as a complex, extensive, and transcendent "watchful world."[5] The rituals of renewal examined in this chapter were infused by these meaning structures. In addition, we have seen that there were structures of meaning that suggested that ritual processes actually reconstituted the animals that were killed. In this sense, Northern Plains peoples believed that the animals upon which they depended for food were, in principle, inexhaustible.

But this belief was not taken lightly, since there were many powerful Others at work who could, should they choose, remove the animals from the people. Indeed, the animals themselves could band together and decide to withdraw themselves from the human beings. These meanings infused the work of renewal with an additional level of seriousness and ensured that rituals were carefully and properly enacted. Because of these supporting meaning structures, the belief that the animals could be renewed did not lead to the idea that, because they were inexhaustible, hunting could proceed in an unrestrained manner. On the level of practice, behavior was further shaped by the negative example of Trickster's foolish or wasteful hunting (see Grinnell 1962: 158; Harrod 1987: 54–65).[6]

What is more difficult and in some cases impossible to recover are the broader meanings that surrounded the theme of renewal in Northern Plains Sun Dances. There clearly were beliefs about the connections between human action and the renewal of animals. In the discussion of the construction of Sun Dance altars, for example, it seems that the people believed that the process of construction was associated with the emergence of a renewed world. What was done on the human level was necessarily connected, therefore, to what occurred in the wider context of what we would understand to be the "natural world." But the desired effects were not forthcoming as a consequence of an automatic or mechanistic causal connection. Rather, the emergence of the desired consequences was dependent upon maintaining or reestablishing appropriate relationships with transcendent Others. So the petitions of the people, the intentions that informed their ritual processes, were directed toward personal agents whose powers could be called upon and, given past experience, whose action on behalf of the people could be counted on.

There was always the sense, however, that dangers were involved. Transcendent Others had cognizance of what the human beings were doing and knew whether their ritual behavior was appropriate. If it was not, then there was the real possibility that the animals would be withheld, and the people would suffer, even starve. Again, the oral traditions provided many examples of predecessors who were portrayed as being in such a condition because they made mistakes in ritual behavior or otherwise gave offense to masters of the animals or animal spirits. Memories of the plight of these predecessors provided an additional context of meaning that surrounded and informed ritual actions.[7]

While ritual aspects surrounding the disposition of bones of slaughtered animals were not as extensive compared to the northern and northeastern Algonquians (cf. Speck 1935; Tanner 1979; Brightman 1993), buffalo skulls and hides certainly played a prominent role in Northern Plains Sun Dances as well as other ceremonies. It was clear in the case of the Arapaho Sun Dance, for example, that we are dealing with actions that involved the modeling of a living animal. The Dorsey text described a ritual hunt, and there were beliefs concerning the presence of the animal's life-element in the hide. Furthermore, there were beliefs that, through ritual processes, the life-element could be renewed. Given these cultural meanings, it is appropriate to interpret the ritual hunt and slaughter, along with the consequent reassembly of the animal, as powerful symbolic acts that were believed to issue in the actual renewal of the buffalo.

As indicated above, buffalo skulls were also pervasive in Northern Plains rituals of renewal. My reading of traditions and descriptions of ritual processes featuring buffalo skulls has suggested the hypothesis that they were experienced as charged with the animal's life principle or "soul." This was explicitly stated by Walker in his interpretation of the Lakotas. Generalizing this hypothesis allows us to account for the powerful experiences that accompanied the widespread use of buffalo skulls in rituals. It is interesting to note that the Mandans had similar beliefs about the skulls of human predecessors; these skulls were often arranged in circles outside the villages and were places where relatives would visit and communicate with their deceased family members (see Catlin 1973, 2: 89–91). Likewise, what were believed to be the skulls of culture heroes were included in important Mandan and Hidatsa bundles (Bowers 1963. 342). The belief that the person and his or her "power" resided in the skull and could be accessed through rituals that featured this body part seems also to have been widely extended to the buffalo.

Relationality and Cultural Convergence

While the evolutionary paradigm characterizes the present experience of many non-Indian people in North America, the world experience of Northern Plains peoples was based upon the assumption that the powers who supported (or failed to support) life were personal. The process of acquiring knowledge in such a world was grounded upon this assumption. The characteristically close observation of animal behavior, of plants, and of the complex features of the natural world so prominent among Northern Plains peoples was thus intertwined with the expectation that distinctive transcendent powers could communicate with human beings. As we have seen, much of this communication took place in the dream and vision experiences that were not only sought after but at times spontaneously irrupted in human experience.

The cultural assumptions that were evident in rituals of renewal were religious in the sense that they sought to give meaning to experiences that were essential for life but were ultimately shrouded in mystery. Central among these experiences was the relation between human beings and other life forms, particularly the animals and plants upon which the people depended for food. The Northern Plains cultural taxonomies that were developed to portray this relationship were grounded in oral traditions concerning origins, culture heroes, and a complex of richly imagined animal traditions. These traditions generated cultural meanings that configured experience and performed functions similar to contemporary explanations based either on creationism or on an evolutionary perspective.

The meanings that constituted Northern Plains experiences of animals, plants, and other aspects of the natural world were clearly different from those that characterize contemporary creationism or evolutionary hypotheses. "Creationism" is a term that describes the view that the universe and all of life arose as a consequence of the activities of a transcendent being who is essentially associated with the Judeo-Christian and Muslim traditions. In most versions of this view, human beings are granted clear priority and greater value than animals, which are understood as having been created for the benefit of humankind, which therefore has legitimate dominion over them.

Evolutionary hypotheses vary and are often contested, but their consequences for constituting experiences of animals and plants in the everyday world can be generally characterized. Central to many of these perspectives is the framing of the emergence of the human being on a very broad canvas. This canvas often includes notions concerning the deep interconnection of all life forms as well as the complexity, mystery, and sometimes seemingly arbitrary character of the evolutionary process.[8] Northern Plains world apprehensions also focus in their own way upon ideas of interconnection, complexity, mystery, and the dangerous arbitrariness that often characterizes the transcendent powers.

In addition to these surprising examples of cultural convergence, there was also the notion among Northern Plains peoples that not only do human beings live in a world populated by transcendent Others but these Others could, by their own powers or by their control of other powers, produce the rhythmic renewal of the world. There is a similar notion, based upon the paradigm of ecological science, that informs some non-Indian reflections on the environment. This notion, which is sometimes constructively related to an evolutionary paradigm, is essentially the view that the natural world possesses broad, self-renewing capacities. From this perspective, environmental problems are ultimately related to a dangerous lack of fit that has developed between human beings and the rest of nature. Rather than living within nature and seeing humankind as deeply a part of nature, many contemporary societies have turned the natural world into a cultural artifact, subordinating it radically for human use.[9]

The United States is clearly an example of such a society. Along with other highly industrialized societies, the United States has created a culture that leads to the commodification of almost all possible experiences. The natural world has become the ultimate commodity, the resource upon which a vast and complex social world has been erected. The expansion of this social world is fueled by a restless cultural dynamic that is expressed in endless cycles of production and consumption. These cycles are voracious and require that larger and larger dimensions of the natural world be dominated in order to satisfy cultural hungers that are, in principle, unsatisfiable.

The dangers of this dominant culture and the violence it has done and continues to do to the natural world, through both its social organizations and its economic structures, have led to an examination of the traditions of Native American predecessors. I contend that their cultural imagination, along with its powerful rituals and symbolic forms, ought to be an essential ingredient in any projection of cultural visions that purport to guide us—Euro-Americans, African Americans, Native Americans, Asian Americans, and Hispanic Americans—into the twenty-first century. The inclusion of Native American traditions, both present and past, in such a cultural vision will have implications for the emergence of new understandings and new patterns of relations between humans and nonhuman life forms. It is the task of the last chapter to address these concerns.

humans

and

animals

in the

twenty-first

century

Northern Plains peoples created multi-layered world pictures that were legitimated by their oral traditions, and they constructed ritual processes that linked their everyday activities with powerful nonhuman Others. These oral traditions and ritual processes changed through time, but the versions embodied in texts collected by anthropologists and other early observers have allowed us to reimagine them at least in fragmentary form. What has been uncovered in this interpretive reimagining are Northern Plains understandings of appropriate human relations with animals, plants, and the nonhuman world at large—a sacred ecology.[1] The purpose of this final chapter is to bring these complex relations into bolder relief and to elaborate their meaning for contemporary human-animal relations.

It is not easy to assay the broader cultural significance of these richly imagined relationships with animals. In recent times the claim has been made, by both Indians and non-Indians, that Native American "traditional" relationships with the natural world might have direct implications for present thinking by non-Indians about environmental problems. I tend to agree with those who argue that, whatever the implications may be, they are certainly not direct.[2] The dangers of trying to make direct connections are many, but three may be mentioned here.

First, Native American oral traditions that embodied the imagination of animals were aspects of a world picture that did not include contemporary concerns for environmental issues. Native American predecessors did not portray the natural world as a separate object of concern, and they did not make the distinction between nature and culture that informs much contemporary thought. What we call the "environment" was for these people composed of powers and persons. Furthermore, they interpreted events in the natural world such as crop failures or unsuccessful hunting as arising from offenses given to animal masters, plant persons, or violations of ritual process.

This fact generates a second problem. When direct appropriations are attempted, they are too often characterized by decontextualized understandings of Native traditions. Usually the traditions are read from either a New Age or an uncritically romantic perspective; they are seldom, if ever, placed within their historical contexts. Thus the richness of Native American relations with animals, plants, and the other powers of the universe remains largely uninterpreted.

Third, direct appropriations by non-Indians run the risk of continuing a tradition of cultural imperialism that is grossly insensitive to the needs and perspectives of contemporary Native American peoples.[3] Why should we in the non-Indian world continue to exploit Native American traditions when it is our own cultural practices that are mainly responsible for the production of present environmental concerns? This is a question raised by many thoughtful people, Indian and non-Indian.

While I am sensitive to this question, I still believe that when interpretation is informed by attitudes of respect and appreciation and when clear cultural differences are acknowledged, then the Northern Plains portrayal of animals and, more generally, the natural world can begin to inform a process characterized not by direct application but by subversive counterimagining.

The remainder of this chapter will engage in such subversion, deconstructing aspects of contemporary cultural experience and reformulating them in the light of the possibilities envisioned in Northern Plains rituals and religious traditions.

Deconstructing Popular Culture

Perhaps the best place to begin is to return to the issues raised in the introduction. There we learned that the contemporary popular cultural imagination is flooded with animal figures and images that appear in both visual and print media. In the case of children, these animal figures sometimes have personal identities and are often imagined as living in societies. It is tempting to draw a direct correspondence between such constructs of the contemporary imagination and the animals portrayed in Northern Plains oral traditions and in doing so to make Native American traditions comparable with contemporary childhood imaginings. While both sets of phenomena are dependent upon the human capacity to create and maintain symbolic systems, there is a critical difference between the contemporary animals of children's imagination and those of our predecessors on the Northern Plains.

That difference lies in the experienced transcendence of the animals and the relations of both dependence and reciprocity that were entailed by this fact. For Northern Plains peoples, animals clearly possessed qualities of intelligence and capacities for action that were analogous to and often greater than the human beings. They were characterized by a quality of transcendence captured in the term "spirit." Animal spirits were also important mediators between the human world and the world of transcendent powers, which included solar, astral, and other beings who gave rise both to the earth and to the human world.

Given this perspective, it is clear that animals had not only religious but also moral standing in the experience of Northern Plains peoples. They were moral agents with whom the people could establish relations of mutual obligation. Fidelity to these obligations meant that life would flourish, but violation of these relations could bring disastrous consequences. Animals also had standing in religious worlds of meaning either as mediators of their own powers or as agents who made possible relations with other transcendent powers.

Perhaps the most potent cultural symbols shaping the majority ethos in the case of adults in North America are those that embody meanings portraying human dominance over the natural world and valuing human capacities to transform elements of that world into products that will serve the human good. This process is projected into a future that is often imagined as being without limits. This utilitarian ethos has a long history, as we have seen, but its present consequences for the understanding of animals continue to shape both imagination and cultural practices. Let us extend the questions addressed in the introduction by elaborating further the influence of this ethos for understanding both domestic and wild animals.

As it is used here, the distinction between "domestic" and "wild" is culturally specific to contemporary North American society. Domestic animals are those that have become *cultural artifacts*. Within the domestic category there are two broad groups of animals, those closest to us in both proximity and complex relationality and those that become "products" for our use either as food or as sources for other material.

The first group refers to animals that are "pets." These animals are often experienced as having identities, personalities, and needs that are analogous to those of humans. Humans have affection for them, and when they are lost or die they grieve over them. In the interim between their birth and death a whole array of corporate entities produces and sells products to feed and care for these animals. In addition, the professional group that once dealt mainly with domestic food animals—the veterinarians—has expanded to include the highly profitable medical care of millions of dogs, cats, and sometimes more exotic animals as well. Pet cemeteries and insurance are some of the more interesting consequences of this cultural construction.

Pet animals occupy a clear but sometimes precarious place in the human moral universe. We are said to have responsibility for them, we are said to be obligated to treat them with kindness, and we are required to meet their needs for food, shelter, and medical attention. These norms are embodied in laws that prevent cruelty to animals and in regulations that control the use of both types of animals within contexts of medical research. Despite these institutionalized norms, both pet animals and domestic food animals are finally understood to serve human needs. They are often ascribed qualities resembling human personality traits, but the experience of them is radically shaped by the utilitarian ethos. Pet animals may be "cute" and have "sweet" dispositions, but if they soil our houses or bite our neighbors they are brought back into line, often violently. When they are "behaving," they are said to be a comfort to humans who are lonely in an increasingly alienated world. They provide companionship for children, youth, and the elderly, and they still have the reputation of being a human's "best friend." If these animals have been specially bred, they bring status and often money to their owners at the highly financed animal shows that are so widespread in our society. If they are related to sports such as horse or dog racing they can sometimes make their owners quite wealthy. In all of these contexts, however, the animals are reduced to serving often quite trivial human needs.

Especially for humans who live most of their lives in urban contexts, the second kind of animal has become a diminished, shadowy reality. Experiences of the actual slaughter of domestic animals for food are available only to a minority in the U.S. population, and the generation that has memories of such experiences becomes smaller each year. Television and advertising supply our experience with typifications of these animals, but they are so cartoonlike that they obscure from view the systematic and massive slaughter that occurs daily. It is probably impossible for persons even to imagine the amount of blood, feathers, hair, and entrails that are by-products of this killing process. Equally unimaginable is the scale upon which individual animal sentience is confined under "factory farms" and then is efficiently extinguished without thought about the deeper meaning of such acts.

For these reasons, food animals have a mostly shadowy relation to us. The connection between neatly packaged "meat" in the supermarkets and a once-living animal is further obscured by a food culture that has shaped our tastes in a manner that is largely disconnected from a sense of primary relations with the natural world. This generalization applies, of course, not only to animals but to plants as well. The genetic manipulation of both plants and animals is totally focused on the service of human needs. The scientific paradigm that informs this manipulation is increasingly controlled by assumptions that further diminish the possibility that animals will be understood to possess qualities that constitute them as sentient beings with relative autonomy and internal dimensions that are not fully known. Recent experiments with cloning manipulate animals in an increasingly bold manner. In addition, their bodies are genetically modified in order to serve as "better" human food, and their body parts become increasingly important for human use in medical contexts. Notions of their "spirit," their internal complexity, and their religious or moral standing in relation to the human world become increasingly difficult to sustain.[4]

Ritual relations that embody deeper meanings about domestic food animals are radically diminished and, I would argue, sometimes rendered impossible by these cultural practices and the scientific paradigms that inform them. What most people in our society experience is a food culture that includes plants and animals, to be sure. But their deeper status as *sources* is obscured by their transformation into cultural artifacts whose meaning is almost totally disassociated from their status as living beings. For example, living plants and animals have been transformed into "fruit," "vegetables," "grains," and "meat." Sometimes the origin is explicit ("liver," "ham hocks"), but usually it is veiled ("London broil," "hamburger"). Then these products are symbolically classified, uniformly packaged, and often trademarked by corporate entities ("growers" or "processors") as items that have appropriate places within the food culture. The quality of such products is assured by the federal government, and an ever-changing picture of the "nutritional" properties of these foods is provided by continuing scientific research.

This food culture obscures even the indirect relationships with animals and plants that still remain. For example, in the experience of many people, the *source* of these foods becomes the corporate entities that create the symbols that give them meaning and make possible their marketing to customers. The larger background is unclearly imagined, sometimes as a highly managed context for the growth of plants, sometimes as a "farm" where animals dwell under controlled and crowded conditions until they become, through some obscure process, human food.

The food culture that grows out of this context has ritual aspects, to be sure. The ritual consumption of food occurs in many contexts: public occasions such as fairs and political gatherings; institutional contexts such as churches, synagogues, and social clubs; restaurants of many kinds that increasingly emphasize ambience and presentation; and in the homes of "gourmet" cooks as well as in ordinary kitchens that serve the daily needs of family life. The point here is that the food symbols that permeate these rituals and give them meaning are largely disconnected from their sources in the natural world. The corporate entities that produce and market these "foods" have intervened; they and not the natural world are experienced as the sources of these "products."

When plant and animal foods are symbolically associated with the names of the corporations that produce or market them (Armour, Swift, Nabisco, or some other multinational structure), then the corporate entity has tremendous, though not unlimited, power. When combined with information produced by nutritional science, for example, specific foods can be marketed as valuable for their health effects. Furthermore, tastes for foods grown at great distances from the consumer can be established and maintained so that international food marketing becomes a viable and profitable activity. Many consumers are unaware of or uninterested in the country of origin of these "products" and the social and environmental costs that may have been involved in their growth and distribution.

The changing cultural stipulation of tastes for specific products has another interesting dimension: in some parts of our culture steaks and roasts have given way to fish and chicken, butter and cheese have been replaced by a whole array of substitutes, and counterpressures from corporate milk and cattle interests have emerged at the symbolic level through advertising. While the corporate context has significant influence on the way food rituals are both shaped and experienced, they continue to have local and personal meaning. But at this level there is an instability about food rituals that is increasingly unsettling. For example, if a person has appropriated a food culture that includes a chuck roast (prepared as mother did) once a week, then this ritual occasion may be unsettled by the popular counterinformation (presumably backed by "science") that chuck roast clogs the arteries and shortens one's life.

Even more disturbing is the thought that these preferences may arise as a consequence of social construction. While they may have personal, autobiographical roots (mother's chuck roast), they are also deeply intertwined with and partly constituted by the symbolic projections of corporate entities that produce the "meat." Perhaps the most corrosive aspect that lies below all of these considerations is the increasing awareness of the genetic manipulation and scientific forced feeding that shape what enters the food culture.

Native American hunting traditions on the Northern Plains gave rise to a very different food culture, one that ritually connected humans with the deeper sources of their lives. Contemporary ritualized conduct in a food culture based upon images manipulated by advertising and controlled by corporate interests has mythic dimensions, to be sure. But these rituals are finally not completely nourishing at the symbolic level even though certain nutritional needs may be satisfied. By contrast, Northern Plains food cultures were based upon images embodied in symbols that arose out of and were sustained by a structure of belief and practice that was deeply religious. Plant and animal foods were sources, experienced as persons, who transcended the human beings. In transactions filled with tension and danger as well as ritual ecstasy and kinship, they gave their bodies so that the human beings could live.

This perspective seems very important to consider in the light of what has been said above. This is certainly one place where Native American traditions are of significance for all of us. That significance appears not through the colonizing appropriation of these traditions but rather through allowing them to create cognitive and emotional dissonance in our present relations with the plant and animal sources of our lives. Part of that dissonance and discomfort must include a challenge to the power of the utilitarian paradigm and standard science in general, which is embodied in the shared ethos that informs our cultural practices and especially our relationship with the natural world. If animals and plants could be released from their almost total bondage to these paradigms, if their meaning and being could be freed from the production system, then perhaps they could become again, at the experiential level, true *sources* of our lives.

If these sensibilities could be nurtured, then perhaps the domination of corporate images, scientific paradigms, and technological manipulations could be broken. Certainly these realities would not disappear; there will still be corporations and science, and the utilitarian ethos, though weakened, would probably not disappear altogether. But the cultural power that these social structures have to project themselves as sources would be radically modified, which would amount to a significant cultural renovation. Perhaps there would emerge the possibility of creating food cultures and corresponding ritual processes based upon religious sensibilities that would be more deeply nourishing, both in the symbolic and the nutritional senses.

The effects of scientific paradigms and the utilitarian ethos on our experience of nondomestic animals are also pervasive. As we pointed out above, Native Americans on the Northern Plains did not experience the animals they hunted for food as "wild" but rather as powerful beings to whom they were related in complex ways. Furthermore, they were in almost daily proximity to large and small mammals. Birds and insects were their constant companions. For most of us, small mammals appear in our yards, birds roost in our trees, and fish swim in our ponds. Many of them, whether insect or mammal, that are perceived as "pests" are actively exterminated. The same process of controlled relations to plants is maintained, and "weeds" are actively exterminated, at least from our yards and other close surrounding environments.

These relations with small mammals, birds, insects, and plant communities in urban contexts not only illustrate the ethos of dominance and control but have also given rise to highly profitable economic activities. Corporations devote vast resources to the production of food for birds and to equipment to prevent the squirrels from getting this food from the bird feeders.

Most persons in the United States do not have regular and sustained relations with large mammals in their natural habitats, and when deer, raccoons, bears, or mountain lions reappear in suburbia, they become an inconvenience that threatens our conception of life. Direct proximity to such animals is still available in highly controlled environments such as zoos as well as in some of the national parks. In many of these park settings, however, tourists have come to expect that animals such as the bear and wolf will present themselves for viewing at just the appropriate moment, for example, on Tuesday at 3:00 P.M. when I am driving my family along the Going-to-the-Sun road in Glacier National Park. With the emergence of such attitudes, the national

humans and animals

parks have themselves become massive zoos where animals are expected to serve human needs: they must be there for us to photograph, to see, and to experience. And if they do not show themselves, we are disappointed and feel cheated, deprived of the aesthetic and spiritual benefits that such experiences are supposed to bring.

Furthermore, if I hunt, then I expect that the deer, elk, and moose populations will be managed so that I can have a satisfying and productive experience. I may be deeply concerned that the reintroduction or natural resettlement of the wolf may threaten, through predation, my hunting activities. I may become interested in the findings of wildlife biologists concerning predator-prey relationships and may call for policies restraining, for example, wolf predation when my hunting stock of deer, elk, or moose is threatened.[5] If I fish, then I expect that state or federal agencies will be responsible for restocking rivers or lakes that have been fished out.

The utilitarian ethos is clearly revealed in these expectations for experiencing animals in such settings as national parks and sporting contexts. The impulses to dominate and use environments such as national parks and forests are further extended by the powerful images projected by the recreation industry. These highly profitable corporations have developed an array of equipment that increasingly allows people to experience the back country in ways that they could not just a generation ago. And the numbers of people who seek such experiences are increasing yearly. If such activity is for the purpose of hunting or fishing, then a comparable array of gear and weapons is readily available. When the recreation industry is associated with the powerful off-road vehicles that are presently being produced, then the possibilities for dominating once relatively remote environments increase exponentially, and the different kinds of "users" come into conflict, culturally and politically.

As humans come in larger numbers to such places, the state and federal agencies responsible for their management are faced with a number of challenges. Managers of state and federal parks are pressured to allow access to remote places while at the same time they experience counterpressures from environmental organizations as well as from legislation such as the Endangered Species Act to protect animals such as grizzly bears and their habitats.

These pressures are augmented by demands for increased grazing access on federal lands, by timber companies, and by mining interests that wish to extract gold, copper, and coal from areas within national forests or adjacent to national parks. Given these pressures and the attitudes they inform, wild animals and their habitats are absorbed into human culture, subjected to the utilitarian ethos, and interpreted according to commercial needs. Indeed, wild animals are increasingly manipulated by humans through various techniques of scientific "management" and, in the process, come to be experienced as cultural artifacts.

These direct, though increasingly controlled, experiences of nondomestic animals are further infused with a cultural imagination that is deeply shaped by the visual media, both television and movies. The cartoon animals of Walt Disney have been supplemented by warm fantasies such as *Free Willy*. But the premier source for our imaginal experience of wild animals, often in exotic settings, is nature programming on national television. Such programming doubtless contributes to the development of an appreciation of the natural world, especially in the case of children. Even so, nature programming creates a mediated imaginative experience; viewers seldom have direct encounters based on physical proximity with wild animals. Furthermore, nature programming is a cultural construction that requires the manipulation of color, setting, and camera. In some cases, the animals themselves are manipulated through baiting or other techniques. It is unclear, for example, how many predator-prey scenes were filmed in the context of their "natural" occurrence and how many were created through the baiting of a predator with a prey animal.

Ironically, nature programming may further "domesticate" the natural world and its creatures within the human imagination. At the same time, there is a feeling of discomfort that may also be associated with such experiences. An interesting expression of such popular anxiety concerning the domesticated imagination and utilitarian dominance is revealed in recent movies such as *Jurassic Park* and *Lost World*. In these movies, corporate greed manipulates scientific knowledge to replicate long extinct animals, such as dinosaurs, from preserved genetic material. The clear message of these movies is that even though scientific technique may replicate aspects of the natural world, the animals that emerge from such experiments are far from domesticated, and they certainly cannot be dominated. Indeed, they prey on each other and violently kill humans who are attempting to construct a commercially viable "Jurassic Park."

The tensions between scientific manipulation and wildness, while often crudely portrayed in these movies, are certainly real and important to understand. These tensions have emerged within a culture that has actively sought, through human activities, to control much of the natural world. The iron grip of the utilitarian ethos, combined with scientific paradigms, gives rise to attitudes of dominance that hold us firmly and continue to motivate action. As we move through the twenty-first century, we risk the danger of losing the last remnants of wildness—understood as the relative autonomy of aspects of the natural world—not only in North America but in other parts of the world as well.

Reimagining Kinship with Animals

Is it possible to glimpse, in the religious traditions of Northern Plains hunters, elements that can stimulate a new cultural imagination of the natural world, its plants and especially its animals? Let us turn, finally, to this set of considerations. Reimagining the natural world in the light of the challenge of Native American traditions could lead to the dissolution—or at least the weakening or modification—of the cultural symbols that make possible present relations of dominance, manipulation, and control.

In the case of our relations with domestic food animals, the reconstruction of our cultural symbols could begin healing the deep fissures that characterize this dimension of our experience. If we could re-envision our dependence upon both plant and animal life in the natural world, then transformations in the present food culture might become extensive. We could begin to confront at the experiential level the reality that millions of domestic food animals are sacrificed daily so that we in the human world may flourish. Some who confront this reality may be so affected that they commit themselves to a food culture that excludes animal flesh altogether. Indeed, there are those in our society who have already made this judgment. But those who do not take this course of action must find new ways to interpret the massive daily sacrifice of animal life.

Northern Plains religious traditions have suggested that animal beings are complex transcendent others rather than resources, as we would normally understand them within the utilitarian paradigm. In Northern Plains traditions, animal others give themselves to the people for food; by contrast, in our society food animals are already "domesticated," and thus the meanings embodied in the hunting rituals and traditions of our Native American predecessors are unclear for our large and complex society. Imagine, however, what would happen if domestic animals could be reinterpreted and embodied in cultural symbols that constituted the experience of them as sentient others that have relative autonomy and internal complexity. If domestic animals came to be experienced in this manner, then killing them for food would take on additional dimensions of depth.

Reimagining domestic food animals in this way could enrich our experience by allowing us to acknowledge what has been hidden under the massive symbolic structures constituted by corporate entities that control the production and marketing of food. Confronting the fact that sentient animal others are killed in order that we may live could lead to the construction of more adequate rituals that might begin to reshape the broader food culture. Clearly, the almost total disassociation from the natural world that is reflected in existing food rituals is largely responsible for continuing to obscure the deeper meaning of our actions.

Because these animals are so captured and shaped by symbolic structures of the utilitarian paradigm, the manner in which Northern Plains understandings of kinship might challenge the contemporary food culture seems even murkier. Even if we encounter more directly the meanings that surround killing sentient domestic animals for food, can we hope to develop the sensibility that the beings we feed on may be more like us than we might imagine? Northern Plains religious traditions and ritual processes acknowledged both levels of experience: in this cultural construction, animals were transcendent and different, and at the same time they could become human kin. In some of the creation accounts, animals and humans were portrayed as undifferentiated, with differences emerging in response to the activities of creators or other powerful beings. It is not clear whether an analogous cultural symbolism could be constructed. If such were to occur, then the distance that characterizes our present relations with domestic food animals might be replaced by a deeper and more complex reciprocity and sense of dependence.

Following this trajectory is clearly the subject for another study. Such an effort would require a more detailed analysis of how cultural symbols and ritual processes might be reconstructed. An extensive analysis of the implications of such a reconstruction for present economic arrangements would also have to be provided. Rather than extending the analysis, however, the remainder of this chapter addresses issues that surround nondomestic animals in the light of what we have learned from Northern Plains traditions and ritual processes.

In the case of nondomestic animals it is necessary to develop an interpretation that acknowledges their place in the community of life and leads to sustained work to make their place secure among us. Most of us in North America really do not need to hunt nondomestic animals for food, though the recreational hunting culture and the corporate infrastructure that supports it will certainly continue and will be important for some individuals and groups. The problem is not hunting per se but the untrammeled development of places that were once animal habitats with the consequent reduction in their populations, often leading some species to the brink of extinction. If we really wish to make a place for nondomestic animals among us, then how might Northern Plains hunting traditions illuminate our path toward this goal?

The pervasive understanding of kinship between humans and animals has implications that are perhaps clearer for nondomestic animals than was the case for domestic food animals. While the *direct* application of Northern Plains ideas of kinship leads in inappropriate directions (New Age views, sentimental romanticism, cultural imperialism), this idea does express a quality of relationship that is more fitting than the present ethos of dominance, manipulation, and control.[6] In Northern Plains traditions, that relationship was expressed in terms of friendship, erotic love, and duty to one's spouse and family. While a simulacrum of such relationships is portrayed in popular culture in films like *The Lion King,* I have in mind forms of relationship expressed in Northern Plains notions of kinship between humans and animals that trace out more fundamental interconnections.

These relationships, which are more fitting and realistic than any fantasy about a Lion King, have been glimpsed from many contemporary perspectives. That interdependence includes not only what we would understand as sentient life but also the vast communities of organisms that provide a foundation for the emergence and nurturance of sentient life. Also included are the vital processes of the earth, sometimes envisioned as an orb suspended in space that seems, in some profound way, itself to be alive and in the Gaia theory is treated as a single sentient being.

Northern Plains visions of kinship were embedded in ritual processes that expressed a deeply religious apprehension of these interrelationships. As was suggested above, the dominant culture must imagine a new paradigm that would express, through ritual action, the religious significance of these forms of interdependence of life upon life. This reinterpretation could issue in a religiously grounded vision of interdependence that would have continuities with but not be identical to the Northern Plains visions we have examined. The most important continuity would be the notion that we are grounded in a vast community of life that transcends us in space and has almost unimaginable temporal depths. Our human bodies are vital organisms that share a place with other nonhuman bodies. All of these bodies are the field for endless expressions of life, and it is this dance of life that constitutes the profound kinship among all of us.

Northern Plains peoples believed that animals were kin, but they also believed that animals were different from humans. They had their own societies, their own territories, indeed their own worlds. This insight has deep meaning for our present situation as we move into the world of the twenty-first century. That world, which is presently coming to meet us, may include the further erosion of animal worlds (their complex interrelationships) as well as the territories that are their habitats, their "homes."

If we allow this to occur, then all of the humans who remain on the earth will be greatly diminished. They would have lost, indeed would have destroyed, one of their deepest and longest relationships. They would have created a place for themselves, but would it be more secure? More interesting? More satisfying? I think not, for without the difference that animal life in all its forms brings, and without the interdependencies that our lives together express, human forms of life would surely be greatly impoverished.

These considerations lead to a strong argument, based in part on religious grounds, not simply for the "protection" of nondomestic animal habitats but also for the selective withdrawal of humans from these places. While this proposal may seem to be excessively radical, it is necessary if sensibilities concerning the complex interrelationships between humans and nondomestic animals are to be recovered. If these sensibilities are not nurtured, then relationships with these animals will continue to be totally reduced to a single ethos of dominance and control. If all life other than the human is domesticated, drawn into human culture to be defined and experienced only as cultural artifacts, then the consequence of such a development would be the emergence of a "wild" human—dangerously spiritually diminished, feeding upon life without reflective awareness, destroying life without benefit of the transcendence of conscience.

Some of the powerful forces arrayed against the proposal of selective withdrawal have already been mentioned: the zoolike mentality associated with our national parks, the scientific management of wildlife and habitats, the powerful and profitable recreation industry, the logging and extractive industries, and the pervasive utilitarian ethos that informs these activities. This ethos is embodied in the words of a sign posted at the boundary of the Flathead National Forest in Montana: "A Land of Many Uses." The basic notion articulated in this sign—multiple use—rests directly on a more deeply taken-for-granted utilitarian paradigm. While multiple use may be desirable in many areas of North America, it cannot apply everywhere if we are to preserve the possibility of recovering a reciprocal relationship with nondomestic animals, including birds. The literal transformation of the environment into a commodity, the pressures to consume it recreationally, aesthetically, and materially are too powerful for "multiple use" to be an adequate guide for reimagining our relationships with the natural world.

Logging, mining, grazing, intense recreational pressures, and the movement of population into areas of previously homesteaded private land are all vital forces operating in the present. These elements cannot continue to coexist in areas where large mammals such as the wolf, grizzly bear, and mountain lion are present or have been reintroduced. The cycles of predation required for their sustenance and the critical mass required for their reproduction and genetic diversity cannot long be sustained if all of these forces, though somewhat regulated, are present. Though they have been intensely studied, their movements tracked by radio collar, the knowledge gained will not prevent the decline of habitat and the ultimate demise of these animal populations.[7]

If we are to recover a deeper sense of interrelationship with all nonhuman forms of life, including the domestic animals and plants we consume as food, then we must acknowledge their *transcendence* and their *difference*. This revisioning would be expressed in religious sensibilities concerning our final dependence upon an ultimately mysterious life process that is variously embodied in the human imagination through oral and written traditions as well as through ritual processes. In this manner, those of European origin in North America may begin to recover a sense of kinship with the animals. In the case of nondomestic animals, this sense of kinship must move through a process of separation in order to be reconstituted in a manner that is fundamentally reciprocal.

In order to break the cycle of utilitarianism and scientific management, a certain number of areas must be designated where animal and plant communities can develop without human domination and control. Present "wilderness" designations are inadequate precisely because they call attention to such areas and attract increasingly heavy recreational use. Likewise, the Wild and Scenic River Act has had the ironic consequence of attracting large numbers of tourists who come to raft, fish, or camp along these waters.[8] The pressure on fish populations has led to "stocking," which means, finally, that rivers will become dominated by the human desire to use them in these various ways. Some better way must be found.

If we set aside areas that would be free from human use, then over time animal, bird, and plant communities might recover some of their former cycles of interaction.[9] They would gradually free themselves from the cultural bondage to which we have subjected them, and they would again be perceived as both transcendent and different in relation to the humans. It is at this point, when sensibilities concerning their autonomy and internal complexity are recovered, that a new relationship with the natural world could emerge. Separation could lead to a renewed capacity to love the world and all of its life forms, not perhaps in the erotic ways that characterized our predecessors on the Northern Plains, but not excluding eros either.

Such renewed relationships might heal the deep cultural fissures that presently afflict our relations with the nonhuman animal companions with whom we now interact in such destructive ways. If we could somehow reimagine our relations to these animal others, recovering a sensibility that we share with them sentience, life, and a common home, then perhaps we could more deeply apprehend, as did the Hidatsas, the primordial source from which "the animals came dancing." And we could join this dance of life in the knowledge that all of us—humans and nonhumans—are bound together by networks that feel more like kinship than we could ever have imagined before we encountered the sacred ecology of our Native American predecessors.

epilogue

It was dusk in northwestern Montana. My wife, Annemarie, and I were having an early dinner, enjoying the fading alpine glow on the mountains and the deepening greens of the surrounding lodgepole and larch forest, when a slight movement caressed my peripheral vision. As I turned to look out the back door of the cabin, I was transfixed by the sight of a fully grown mountain lion standing no more than twenty-five yards away. Both of us quickly rose and quietly moved to the door for a better look. As we gazed over that short distance, the big cat slowly turned his head and showed us his full face, returning our gaze with seemingly quiet uninterest. As our eyes remained locked in a mutual gaze, the distance between ourselves as human animals and this great predator seemed to collapse. He may have just finished a meal; we were in the midst of a dinner that included animal flesh. We were products of the same wondrous evolutionary process. Though we seemed to possess a different form of embodied consciousness, this great animal had evolved within his own special sentient world. In this world the lion seemed, to recall Henry Beston's words, "finished and complete, gifted with extensions of the senses we have lost or never attained, living by voices we shall never hear." This thought was interrupted by the turning of the lion's head, which was immediately followed, in a flow of rippling muscles, by its lithe body. He then began a leisurely stroll away from the cabin and down the driveway, where, upon reaching the forest, he disappeared from view. We were left alone with a question that germinated and finally grew into this book: will wild animals and the natural contexts that are their homes accompany us through the twenty-first century?

notes

Animals and Cultural Values

1. The view that the world emerges in experience as a process of human construction is influenced by a variety of sources, the most important of which for this analysis are Schutz (1967), Schutz and Luckmann (1973, 1989), Berger and Luckmann (1966), and Berger (1967).

2. I have also tried to acknowledge the deeper problems that accompany any such analysis. For example, attempts to retrieve Native American traditions on the basis of the vast ethnographic record produced in the late nineteenth and early twentieth centuries must deal with perspectives such as those articulated by Edward Said, whose work provides a brilliant analysis of the consequences of colonialism in a world context. See especially Said (1979, 1994). Said's work has implications for contemporary discussions of the "colonization" of American Indians that have been drawn out with often devastating clarity in the work of Indian scholars such as Vine Deloria Jr. (whose reflections on some of these issues predate Said's work) and Ward Churchill. See especially Deloria (1969) and Churchill (1996, 1992). Some recent anthropological work reflects these sensitivities, especially when such writing is influenced by postmodernist perspectives. See especially Clifford and Marcus (1986) and Marcus and Fischer (1986).

From the perspective of some of these scholars, the continued use of nineteenth- and early-twentieth-century ethnography continues colonial oppression in a very precise sense: the representations of Native American peoples projected on the basis of these ethnographic materials were produced by non-Indian interpreters and are largely still controlled and manipulated by non-Indian interpreters. Thus in a profound sense the oppression continues. While I wish to acknowledge the force of Said's arguments as well as the powerful critiques of Deloria and Churchill, I do believe that there was a complicated and ironic social and moral situation that pertained during the period when the bulk of the ethnographic observations that constitute data for this book were recorded. Certainly the ethnographic record reveals the academic perspectives, cultural prejudices, and human weaknesses of the anthropologists who constructed this material. Certainly field work during the late nineteenth and early twentieth centuries was done under conditions of conquest and suppression of Native American religions, languages, and cultures. In these fundamental senses, this work was and is implicated in the process of domination and marginalizing American Indians.

Even so, out of this maelstrom of pain and extended cultural suffering endured by Native American societies there emerged work, by non-Indians to be sure, that recorded details of the languages as well as the religious and cultural traditions that constituted aspects of the richness of these societies. This fact is as important as it is ironic. Certainly the work of physical anthropologists and others that issued in the collection of human remains and the work of cultural anthropologists that issued in the artifacts collected in museums raise serious moral and legal problems that must be dealt with. Public Law 101–601, the Native American Graves Protection and Repatriation Act, has begun to address the thorny problems of repatriation of human remains and museum artifacts. This important process must continue.

It still seems to me, perhaps naively, that the oral traditions and other cultural descriptions that I work with in this book ought to be available for creative—and subversive—reinterpretation by both Indians and non-Indians alike. I believe that Indian people can turn to this past, though ambiguous, record and find there materials for contemporary cultural renewal. Indeed, Native American people can often find in these earlier materials strong confirmation of their present oral traditions. Conversely, present oral traditions can also correct, expand, and enrich this earlier record.

Likewise, non-Indian interpreters can make their own contributions—if they engage the materials respectfully—by seeking to show forth the richness, beauty, and depth of these cultures and communicating these details to a largely ignorant or romantically inclined majority society. In my view, these are still important tasks, and I hope that this book furthers them in a helpful way.

3. An early exploration of some of the problematical features of Western culture in relation to the environment that included a focus on biblical traditions was written by White (1967). A more recent analysis of Western traditions in relation to environmental issues is by Merchant (1980). See also McFague (1997).

4. Scholars of the Hebrew Bible have also contributed illuminating analyses that propose alternate readings that seek to soften or undercut completely the accepted notion that "dominion" was given to "man" over the animals and other life forms. The tendency of this scholarship is to argue that "dominion" cannot mean the exploitation and manipulation of the natural world strictly for human aggrandizement. See Knight (1985).

5. The classical locus for this view of animals is found in Descartes, *Discourse on Method,* pt. 5. See Descartes (1960: 31–44).

6. See Bentham (1961) and Mill (1957).

7. I will return to these issues in the last chapter. A book that has profoundly influenced my understanding of the emerging consciousness and cultural values that constitute the "touristic experience" is MacCannell (1989).

8. Humans have always interacted with animals, plants, and other features of the natural world in culturally specific ways. Humans have had domestic animal companions during most of their long journey, and they have exploited the sources of the natural world for food and other necessities. The exponential growth of population during the last two centuries, however, has created an entirely new prospect. It may be that the "natural" world will give way almost completely to the domination of human culture. Animals and plants and their "natural" contexts may become zones of manipulation in the service of human needs. If this occurs, then the experience of the "transcendence" of the natural world will fade from human experience. Ironically, the fact that humans are a part of and not apart from the natural world is built into the deep structure of their animal bodies and appears decisively as they approach their limit: death. Ironically, the end of an individual human life condenses the often forgotten meanings that connect all of us to our earthbound home, and in contemplating death we have the possibility of understanding that we, along with other animals, share a common finite life energy.

Chapter 1. Northern Plains Hunters

1. Translation problems and variations in the history of usage by non-Indian scholars surround the names of Indian groups. Many designations obscure internal variation and historical changes, many names are based on inaccurate or inadequate translations from Indian languages, and most names reflect usages standardized by the dominant culture, for example, "Sioux." While I realize that it is less than satisfactory,

I have generally followed conventional usages and spellings in order not to overburden the text. A brief discussion of the term "Blackfeet" will give a general sense of this problem, however. The *Blackfeet* Reservation is the official designation for the reservation in Montana. Some Blackfeet have argued that the translation of Siksika should be *Blackfoot*. And in some of the earlier anthropological accounts, this is in fact the term used. This debate is not settled, however, and I have chosen to use the official designation when referring to the reservation, the term "Blackfeet" when referring to the people as a whole, and the term "Blackfoot" as the adjectival form of the proper noun.

2. The social and religious changes that these groups endured formed the subject of my most recent book (Harrod 1995).

3. Frison has detailed descriptions of the precautions that must have been taken in order to preserve the meat if a kill had to be left for any length of time. For example, if a single hunter was involved, he would have to gut the animal and then prop open its body cavity in order for proper cooling to occur, especially in warm weather. Furthermore, if the hunter had to leave the carcass overnight, then it was in danger of being consumed by predators. Communal hunting did not present these kinds of problems since butchering took place either at the kill site or a short distance away, and the meat and other products were processed within a short time period.

Chapter 2. In the Beginning There Were Animals

1. The adaptability and creativity exhibited in the formation of new cultural identities can be traced among several Northern Plains peoples who were migrants from the east and northeast and who became buffalo hunters during the course of their westward movements. I have dealt with these issues in my latest book (Harrod 1995; cf. Harrod 1987).

2. Interpretive categories used in this and the following chapter, such as *creator* and *trickster, animal master* and *culture hero,* are not entirely adequate. They have been developed by anthropologists, folklorists, and historians of religion and are often too general to capture the unique features of the beings who have specific identities in particular traditions. They do indicate functions, however, that seem to characterize each type. And I think that the persistence of these figures and functions indicates that they were pervasive elements of religious world pictures that were widespread in North America.

3. Indigenous categories also organized other sorts of experience, such as dreams. For example, the Crows divided dreams into four categories: ordinary dreams, dreams of the future, property dreams, and dreams of power. Crows understood dreams of power to be the most important of these visionary categories (Wildschut 1960: 5–6).

4. These Blackfoot phrases come from the texts produced by Uhlenbeck (1912: 5; 1913: 1). See Franz and Russell's more recent Blackfoot dictionary for examples of contemporary transliteration and spelling.

5. Analyses of the earth diver traditions have been featured in the work of historians of religion who have been influenced by Mircea Eliade. While this work is interesting, I find it somewhat too disconnected from particular cultural meanings to be useful for the present analysis.

6. Wissler reported a similar statement: "I have heard the Piegan say that so and so 'must be trying to be like the Old Man; he cannot be trusted with women'" (Wissler and Duvall 1908: 10).

7. There were typical variations in these accounts. For example, in one of them (Dorsey 1903: 3–4) the creator figure was portrayed as floating on the water on a flat pipe along with his wife and a male child.

8. Interpretations of Lakota origin traditions are fraught with debate. For some of these discussions, see Melody (1977), Jahner (1987), Powers (1977), and Walker (1983: 1–40). Despite the textual, methodological, and interpretive problems, I will reconstruct elements of Lakota origin traditions in order to show how they seem to have portrayed the relation between humans and animals.

9. There were other creation accounts written for a popular audience, an example of which would be Eastman (1911: 119–44). This story included both a creator and a culture hero figure as well as a discussion of the relation between humans and the animals. In this tradition, Iktomi (Spider) undermined the original kinship relation between the first human and the animals. A conflict ensued and was resolved when the animal people agreed, through a treaty, that they would furnish the human beings their skins and fur for clothing and their bodies for food.

Chapter 3. The Gift of Animals

1. We have seen that game animals were also represented in the narratives as possessing the qualities of agency: they were *persons* who had purposes, will, language, and power. In this sense, some Northern Plains oral traditions conformed to Hallowell's more general assessment concerning the experience of indigenous peoples in North America: "Animals are believed to have essentially the same sort of animating agency which man possesses. They have a language of their own, can understand what human beings say and do, have forms of social or tribal organization, and live a life which is parallel in other respects to that of human societies" (1926: 7). However, some traditions on the Northern Plains did not fit so nicely under this generalization. For example, while the Cheyennes, Hidatsas, Arikaras, Lakotas, and Pawnees apparently had traditions concerning animal agency, there is some evidence to suggest that

the Assiniboines did not believe animals possessed such powers (Hultkrantz 1953: 491–92). This problem is far from solved, and while the present chapter addresses it, no final conclusions will be drawn on the matter.

2. This gift would be transferred to the Cheyenne people as a consequence of Sweet Medicine's return to the mountain. After he had married a chief's daughter the two of them set out for the Black Hills. When they reached the mountain they entered and were given four arrows by the beings who were inside. Through the arrows and an associated ritual process the people gained power not only over the buffalo but over their enemies as well. Chapter 4 explores the ritual of the Sacred Arrows in greater depth.

3. The tradition points out that because human flesh had become a part of the buffalo, the Arikaras would discard the meat from under the buffalo's shoulder.

4. Because the Arikaras were kinspersons with the Pawnees, they shared many traditions. For a similar Arikara tradition, see Hawk's narrative in Dorsey (1904a: 94–101).

5. Another type of tradition that differs from those discussed in this chapter appeared among the Crows (Lowie 1918: 216–18). This tradition described a society of giants who lived underground and used buffalo as their horses. Four Crow men were out hunting, and they followed buffalo tracks until they came to the mouth of a cave. They passed through the cave and came into the country of the giants who did not know how to use either bows and arrows or guns. The Crows were able to obtain a large herd of buffalo from the giants, and, when they passed through the cave, the buffalo followed them. The four men traveled back toward their people with the animals following, and from that time on the Crows had plenty of buffalo in their country.

Chapter 4. Animal Rituals on the Northern Plains

1. Rituals featuring buffalo were enacted in areas beyond the Northern Plains, as Howard reminds us:

> Buffalo dances were widespread in eastern North America and the Midwest, reminding us that the range of the bison was not limited to the High Plains. Dances honoring the buffalo were performed by the Mohawk, Oneida, Onondaga, Cayuga, Seneca, Delaware, Shawnee, Cherokee, Choctaw, Creek, Yuchi, Seminole, Calusa, Ojibwa, Fox, Sauk, Potawatomi, Winnebago, and Eastern Dakota, and probably other "Woodland" groups as well. Continuing west, we find that dances and ceremonies honoring the buffalo were universal in the Prairie and High Plains regions. All of the eastern Pueblo tribes have buffalo dances, and even the Hopi

have a Buffalo kachina. Certain Plateau groups, such as the Flathead and Nez Perce, and Great Basin groups such as the Bannock and Shoshone, also have buffalo dances or include buffalo symbolism in major tribal rites. (1974: 241)

Bear rituals have been extensively discussed by Hallowell (1926), and references to other animal rituals such as those focused on smaller game are widespread.

2. Some of these oral traditions such as the Sweet Medicine and Erect Horns narratives were introduced in the previous chapter.

3. Reinterpretation is also the ground out of which have grown the myriad contemporary projects of cultural renaissance and resistance among Northern Plains peoples. For example, the smoking of the pipe, the sweat lodge, and many rituals that previously focused upon hunting have been transformed into practices that address the needs of contemporary peoples. If non-Indian people begin to understand things from this point of view, then they will grasp the fact that many Indian people have not "assimilated" but rather are still deeply embedded in cultural patterns, values, and religious practices that have old, though often reinterpreted, roots. For an analysis that describes the cultural dynamic of tradition and innovation in relation to a particular ritual process, see Bucko (1998).

4. Buffalo rocks were typically ammonites or baculites but could also simply be strangely shaped pieces of stone or flint. See Wissler (1912: 243) and Grinnell (1962: 126).

5. The artist Bob Scriver, who still lives and works on the reservation, had a very extensive collection of Blackfoot bundles and other "artifacts," some of which were collected by his father in the early twentieth century. In response to contemporary repatriation pressures, Scriver sold his collection to the Provincial Museum of Alberta in Canada. For photographs of the contents of beaver and other Blackfoot bundles, see Scriver (1990: 208–37, 258–81).

6. There were many tipis upon which were painted the images of animals and other powerful persons such as Sun, Moon, and Morningstar. The images on these tipis were given to their original owners through a vision experience, but they could be and were transferred from one person to another; in this sense, painted tipis were "bundles" that gave their owners access to the particular forms of power associated with the beings who were represented on them. For photographs, see Scriver (1990: 134–45).

7. This description follows both Schlesier (1987) and Grinnell (1972, vol. 2). Schlesier's interpretations are based on his experiences with contemporary Cheyenne ritual specialists. For this reason, he views his interpretation as "correct." I am making no such claims, but I do believe that the Massaum can reasonably be viewed as I have interpreted it in this chapter.

8. The descriptions included in this chapter focus mainly upon the Skidi band, which may have had as many as thirteen villages and was united into a political confederacy.

9. Among the Skidi Pawnee, the Evening Star bundle was superior, and four "leading bundles," the Yellow Star, Red Star, White Star, and Big Black Meteoric Star, followed in importance. Each of these bundles had a "priest" who conducted the ritual, but the Evening Star bundle was the source of most of the ritual content for the others (Murie 1984: 13).

10. The burning of bones is reminiscent of the practice of scapuluimancy among the northern Algonquians, although there is no evidence here that the bones were "read" in order to gain information about game animals. See Speck (1935: chap. 6).

11. This tradition was recorded by Clark Wissler and incorporated into Walker's description of Sioux games.

12. Age-graded societies for both men and women were widespread on the Northern Plains. See Wissler (1916) and Stewart (1977: pt. 2, chap. 2).

13. Women's dances that were not associated with age-graded societies, such as a dance among the Arapahoes, were also evident among Northern Plains societies (Kroeber 1902).

14. Buffalo masks constructed in much the same manner were used in Plains Cree dances (Skinner 1914: 530–31). The Mandans, Hidatsas, and other groups used similar masks in their animal dances as well.

15. The organization of communal hunts took a similar form in many buffalo-hunting societies in North America. For an example of such an organization among the Ojibwas and the Pawnees, see Skinner (1914: 494–99) and Murie (1914: 557).

16. For additional material on the white buffalo among the Lakotas, see Fletcher (1884).

17. Contemporary Cree hunters illustrate these themes, and their language clearly associates hunting with sexual intercourse (Brightman 1993: 127–32). Among the Yup'ik Eskimos, maintaining appropriate relations between the genders is essential to successful hunting (Fienup-Riordan 1994: chap. 5).

Chapter 5. Renewing the Animals

1. Wissler has commented that "the seminal idea in the whole [ritual] complex is the spring revival of life. No matter whether the rituals and ceremonial objects have to do with plants or animals, each spring their powers must be renewed with appropriate ceremonies; and again in the winter all must be relegated to a symbolic sleep" (quoted in Murie 1984: 465).

2. The altar constructed in the Arapaho Sun Dance lodge was very similar in ap-

pearance and featured a painted buffalo skull surrounded by earth as well as live foliage. This altar was also symbolically associated with the renewal of the buffalo (Dorsey 1903: 118–19, and see plate LXI for a color representation of this altar).

Among both the Cheyennes and the Arapahoes, the wife of the man who had pledged the Sun Dance had intercourse with the ritual leader. For the Cheyennes, this woman had become identified with Erect Horn's companion and the ritual leader with the culture hero himself. As a part of the Arapaho Sun Dance, the same act probably occurred between the lodge-maker's wife and the ritual leader (Dorsey 1905b: 130–31; 1903: 172–78). I interpret these acts to be deeply symbolic of the renewal of the fecundity of the earth as well as contributing to the fertility of the people themselves.

3. The buffalo ritual was given to the Lakotas by one of the Buffalo Women. It was a ritual that involved young women who had experienced their first menstruation. Some analyses of this ritual associate it with the maintenance of male power over women. See, for example, Walker (1982b: 241–53).

4. The groups that tied a buffalo hide to the Sun Dance center pole included the Crows, Arapahoes, Lakotas, Arikaras, Hidatsas, Assiniboines, Sisseton Dakotas, and Canadian Dakotas (Spier 1921: 466).

5. This term is borrowed from a chapter title in Nelson (1983: 14).

6. When the buffalo were finally exterminated from the Northern Plains, many groups continued for a time to believe that either the animals had chosen to withdraw or that an animal master had cached them in a cave. As these beliefs gradually faded in the tragic light of reality, Northern Plains peoples entered deeper into an experience of economic exploitation and cultural depression from which some groups continue to suffer.

7. It does not really matter whether the narratives concerning predecessors portrayed "real" historical events; their meaning-effect was the same.

8. The literature is immense, but I have particularly in mind books like Gould (1989), Thomas (1974), and Eisley (1970). Loren Eisley's *Darwin's Century* is a wonderful overview of the historical emergence of the idea of evolution.

9. For a popular rendition of this perspective, see McGibben (1989). For a "tougher" view of the capacities of the natural world to withstand human depredations, see Lovelock (1979).

Chapter 6. Humans and Animals in the Twenty-First Century

1. For a more general description of the "cosmography" of the Great Plains as a whole, see Irwin (1994: chap. 3). Irwin's term includes elements of what I am calling in this book a "sacred ecology."

2. While his case is somewhat overstated, an example of some of the arguments I have in mind appears in Martin (1978: 157–88). The analysis in the previous chapters has clearly shown that what might be called the "ethno-ontology" of Northern Plains peoples constituted a basic world picture that cannot directly be compared with or translated into the symbolic structures that form the ethos of contemporary North American society. Nevertheless, I still believe that in the United States those of European descent must attend to their own ethos; but I also believe that that ethos can constructively be challenged by the traditions of Native American predecessors. I have tried in this book to walk along this difficult path.

3. For a biting critique of cultural imperialism, see "A Little Matter of Genocide: Colonialism and the Expropriation of Indigenous Spiritual Tradition in Academia," in Churchill (1996: 315–36); see also Churchill (1992).

4. A pattern of avoidance of thought about the extent to which both plants and food animals are genetically engineered typifies the attitudes of many persons in the United States. Deeper thought about the implications of these manipulations, especially in medical contexts, might present challenges to present notions. The details and conceptual justifications surrounding the use of mice and other animals in medical contexts escape much popular notice. Except for the most extreme animal activists, appeals to the necessity of the "animal model" in medical research, to regulations governing such activities, or to the deeper personal fears concerning disease are usually sufficient to quiet all but the most persistent questions. A more serious consideration of the use of animals genetically programmed to develop cancer would perhaps lever the edges of the genetic paradigm, allowing us to confront directly the implications of such activities. Analyses of costs and benefits might be significantly rethought were this to occur. I am not arguing that such activities could not, for any reason, be justified, but I am arguing that discussion of the implications of such developments should occur in the broader culture in order to evoke a more widespread awareness about the meaning of these activities. For example, what are the larger meanings surrounding the creation of the "OncoMouse," which was put on the market by the Du Pont Corporation in 1989? The advertising of this "animal artifact" in science journals indicated that "each OncoMouse carries the *ras* oncogene in all germ and somatic cells. This transgenic model, available commercially for the first time, predictably undergoes carcinogenesis. OncoMouse reliably develops neoplasms within months . . . and offers you a shorter path to new answers about cancer. Available to researchers only from Du Pont, where better things for better living come to life" (quoted in Fujimura 1996: 7; an image of this animal appears in Fujimura 1996: 8).

5. In addition to complaints by hunters, attitudes expressed by cattle and sheep ranchers toward the wolf reintroduction program in Yellowstone National Park reveal a deep cultural hostility toward this particular predator. Sometimes these attitudes

are translated into actions described by a common phrase heard in the West: "Shoot and shovel."

6. If this perspective were developed more fully in terms of an "environmental ethic," then the notion of the *fitting* would have to be further elaborated. The beginning point for my constructive efforts would be H. Richard Niebuhr's important essay on relational value, "The Center of Value," in Niebuhr (1960: 100–113). Ideally, such a perspective would include a discussion not only of domestic food animals and nondomestic animals but the natural world as a whole. My colleague, Sallie McFague, has begun this task in her book, *Super, Natural Christians* (1997). In this work she addresses herself to the renewal of sensibilities within the Christian tradition that would bear upon a more adequate love of the natural world. Some of Vine Deloria Jr.'s more recent writings on religion also discuss the contemporary relevance of Native American understandings of land and animals. See, for example, his 1991 essay, "Reflection and Revelation: Knowing Land, Places and Ourselves," in Deloria (1999: 250–60).

7. The observation that deer, foxes, coyotes, mountain lions, bears, and other animals can often be seen around small towns and in suburban areas in the western states and elsewhere is often used as evidence to show that these animals are doing very well. Indeed, it is sometimes argued that they are too abundant; a few make the claim that this is evidence that human activity is not harmful, and therefore humans and animals can coexist. While it is true that some deer populations, for example, in suburban areas, have greatly expanded, this fact is due to the lack of natural predators and to the activities of humans, who often feed these animals during especially harsh winters. Furthermore, encounters with bears and mountain lions have often led to fatal outcomes for the humans, which usually leads to a cry to control these animals, even to exterminate them.

8. These areas can be located on the Internet, and commercial outfitting is readily available for groups who wish to visit such places.

9. These areas must be set aside not on the grounds that they will contribute something valuable for the humans, such as material for medical use or increased elitist opportunities for environmental tourism, but rather on the grounds that they are required if humans are to recover more appropriate relationships with animal and plant communities.

bibliography

Beckwith, Martha Warren

1930　*Myths and Hunting Stories of the Mandan and Hidatsa Sioux.* Vassar College Field-Work in Folk-Lore. Poughkeepsie, N.Y.: Vassar College.

1937　*Mandan-Hidatsa Myths and Ceremonies.* American Folk-Lore Society. New York: J. J. Augustin.

Bell, Catherine

1992　*Ritual Theory, Ritual Practice.* New York: Oxford University Press.

Bentham, Jeremy

1961　*An Introduction to the Principles of Morals and Legislation.* New York: Hafner Publishing Company.

Berger, Peter

1967　*The Sacred Canopy: Elements of a Sociology of Religion.* New York: Doubleday.

Berger, Peter, and Thomas Luckmann

1966　*The Social Construction of Reality: A Treatise in the Sociology of Knowledge.* New York: Doubleday.

Beston, Henry

1928　*The Outermost House.* New York: Henry Holt and Company.

Biolsi, Thomas, and Larry J. Zimmerman

1997　*Indians and Anthropology: Vine Deloria Jr. and the Critique of Anthropology.* Tucson: University of Arizona Press.

Boller, Henry A.

1959   *Among the Indians: Eight Years in the Far West, 1858–1866*. Chicago: R. R. Donnelley and Sons.

Bowers, Alfred W.

1950   *Mandan Social and Ceremonial Organization*. University of Chicago Publications in Anthropology, Social Anthropological Series. Chicago: University of Chicago Press.

1965   *Hidatsa Social and Ceremonial Organization*. Smithsonian Institution Bureau of American Ethnology, Bulletin 194. Washington, D.C.: U.S. Government Printing Office.

Brightman, Robert A.

1993   *Grateful Prey: Rock Cree Human-Animal Relationships*. Berkeley: University of California Press.

Brown, Joseph Epes

1992   *Animals of the Soul: Sacred Animals of the Oglala Sioux*. Rockport, Mass.: Element.

Bucko, Raymond A.

1998   *The Lakota Ritual of the Sweat Lodge: History and Contemporary Practice*. Studies in the Anthropology of North American Indians. Ed. Raymond J. DeMallie and Douglas R. Parks. Lincoln: University of Nebraska Press.

Bullchild, Percy

1985   *The Sun Came Down: The History of the World as My Blackfeet Elders Told It*. San Francisco: Harper and Row.

Catlin, George

1967   *O-Kee-Pa: A Religious Ceremony and Other Customs of the Mandans*. Ed. John C. Ewers. New Haven, Conn.: Yale University Press.

1973   *Letters and Notes on the Manners, Customs, and Conditions of North American Indians*. 2 vols. New York: Dover Publications.

Churchill, Ward

1992   *Fantasies of the Master Race: Literature, Cinema and the Colonization of American Indians*. Monroe, Maine: Common Courage Press.

1996   *From a Native Son: Selected Essays in Indigenism, 1985–1995*. Boston: South End Press.

Clifford, James, and George E. Marcus, eds.

1986   *Writing Culture: The Poetics and Politics of Ethnography*. Berkeley: University of California Press.

Cooper, John M.

1957   *The Gros Ventres of Montana. Part II: Religion and Ritual*. Ed. Regina Flannery.

Catholic University of America. Anthropological Series no. 16. Washington, D.C.: Catholic University of America Press.

Deloria, Ella

1932   *Dakota Texts*. Publications of the American Ethnological Society, vol. 14. New York: G. E. Stechert and Company.

Deloria, Vine

1969   *Custer Died for Your Sins*. London: Macmillan Company.

1999   *For This Land: Writings on Religion in America*. Ed. James Treat. New York: Routledge.

Descartes, René

1960   *Discourse on Method and Meditations*. Trans. Laurence J. Lafleur. New York: Bobbs-Merrill Company.

Dorsey, George A.

1903   *The Arapaho Sun Dance: The Ceremony of the Offerings Lodge*. Field Columbian Museum, Publication 75, Anthropological Series 4.

1904a   *Traditions of the Arikara*. Carnegie Institution of Washington, Publication 17. Washington, D.C.: Carnegie Institution of Washington.

1904b   *Traditions of the Skidi Pawnee*. Memoirs of the American Folk-Lore Society 8.

1905a   *The Cheyenne: Ceremonial Organization*. Field Columbian Museum, Publication 99, Anthropological Series, vol. 9, pt. 1.

1905b   *The Cheyenne: The Sun Dance*. Field Columbian Museum, Publication 103, Anthropological Series, vol. 9, pt. 2.

1906   *The Pawnee. Mythology (Part I)*. Carnegie Institution of Washington, Publication 59. Washington, D.C.: Carnegie Institution of Washington.

1907   "The Skidi Rite of Human Sacrifice." *Proceedings of the International Congress of Americanists* 15: 65–70.

Dorsey, George A., and Alfred L. Kroeber

1903   *Traditions of the Arapaho*. Field Columbian Museum, Publication 81, Anthropological Series 5.

Dorsey, James Owen

1894   *A Study of Siouan Cults*. Eleventh Annual Report of the Bureau of Ethnology 1889–90. Washington, D.C.: U.S. Government Printing Office.

Eastman, Charles Alexander

1911   *The Soul of the Indian*. New York: Houghton Mifflin Company.

Eisley, Loren

1958   *Darwin's Century: Evolution and the Men Who Discovered It*. New York: Doubleday and Company.

1970   *The Invisible Pyramid*. New York: Charles Scribner's Sons.

Ewers, John C.

1949   "The Last Bison Drives of the Blackfoot Indians." *Journal of the Washington Academy of Sciences* 39, no. 11: 355–60.

1955   *The Horse in Blackfoot Indian Culture.* Smithsonian Institution, Bureau of American Ethnology Bulletin 159. Washington, D.C.: U.S. Government Printing Office.

1958   *The Blackfeet.* Norman: University of Oklahoma Press.

1967   "Was There a Northwestern Plains Sub-Culture? An Ethnographic Appraisal." *Plains Anthropologist* 36, no. 12: 167–73.

Fienup-Riordan, Ann

1983   *The Nelson Island Eskimo: Social Structure and Ritual Distribution.* Anchorage: Alaska Pacific University Press.

1994   *Boundaries and Passages: Rule and Ritual in Yup'ik Eskimo Oral Tradition.* Civilization of the American Indian Series, vol. 212. Norman: University of Oklahoma Press.

Flannery, Regina

1953   *The Gros Ventres of Montana. Part I: Social Life.* Catholic University of America. Anthropological Series no. 15. Washington, D.C.: Catholic University of America Press.

Fletcher, Alice C.

1884   *The White Buffalo Festival of the Uncpapas.* Sixteenth and Seventeenth Annual Reports of the Trustees of the Peabody Museum of American Archaeology and Ethnology, vol. 3, 3–4.

Franz, Donald G.

1997   *Blackfoot Grammar.* Toronto: University of Toronto Press.

Franz, Donald G., and Norma Jean Russell

1995   *Blackfoot Dictionary of Stems, Roots, and Affixes.* 2nd ed. Toronto: University of Toronto Press.

Frison, George C.

1978   *Prehistoric Hunters of the High Plains.* New York: Academic Press.

Fujimura, Joan H.

1996   *Crafting Science: A Sociohistory of the Quest for the Genetics of Cancer.* Cambridge, Mass.: Harvard University Press.

Gould, Stephen Jay

1989   *Wonderful Life: The Burgess Shale and the Nature of History.* New York: W. W. Norton and Company.

Grinnell, George Bird

1901   "The Lodges of the Blackfeet." *American Anthropologist* n.s. 3: 650–68.

1907   "Some Early Cheyenne Tales." *Journal of American Folk-Lore* 20: 169–94.

1908   "Some Early Cheyenne Tales II." *Journal of American Folk-Lore* 20: 269–320.

1910   "The Great Mysteries of the Cheyenne." *American Anthropologist* n.s. 12: 542–75.

1961   *Pawnee Hero Stories and Folk-Tales.* Lincoln: University of Nebraska Press.

1962   *Blackfoot Lodge Tales.* Lincoln: University of Nebraska Press.

1971   *By Cheyenne Campfires.* Lincoln: University of Nebraska Press.

1972   *The Cheyenne Indians: Their History and Ways of Life.* 2 vols. Lincoln: University of Nebraska Press.

Hallowell, A. Irving

1926   Bear Ceremonialism in the Northern Hemisphere." *American Anthropologist* n.s. 28, no. 1: 1–175.

Harrod, Howard L.

1971   *Mission among the Blackfeet.* Civilization of the American Indian Series, vol. 112. Norman: University of Oklahoma Press.

1987   *Renewing the World: Plains Indian Religion and Morality.* Tucson: University of Arizona Press.

1995   *Becoming and Remaining a People: Native American Religions on the Northern Plains.* Tucson: University of Arizona Press.

Hill, Ruth Beebe

1979   *Hanta Yo.* New York: Doubleday and Company.

Howard, James H.

1974   "The Arikara Buffalo Society Medicine Bundle." *Plains Anthropologist* 19, no. 66: 241–71.

Hubinger, Václav

1996   *Grasping the Changing World: Anthropological Concepts in the Postmodern Era.* New York: Routledge.

Hultkrantz, Åke

1953   *Conceptions of the Soul among North American Indians.* Stockholm: Ethnographical Museum of Sweden, Monograph Series, Publication no. 1.

Hymes, Del

1981   *"In Vain I Tried to Tell You": Essays in Native American Ethno-poetics.* Philadelphia: University of Pennsylvania Press.

Irwin, Lee

1994   *The Dream Seekers: Native American Visionary Traditions of the Great Plains.* Civilization of the American Indian Series, vol. 213. Norman: University of Oklahoma Press.

Jahner, Elaine A.

1987   "Lakota Genesis: The Oral Tradition." In Raymond J. DeMallie and Douglas R. Parks, eds. *Sioux Indian Religion.* Norman: University of Oklahoma Press, 45–65.

Kehoe, Alice Beck

1970   "The Function of Ceremonial Sexual Intercourse among the Northern Plains Indians." *Plains Anthropologist* 15: 99–103.

1981   *North American Indians: A Comprehensive Account.* Englewood Cliffs, N.J.: Prentice-Hall.

Kehoe, Thomas F.

1967   "The Boarding School Bison Drive Site." *Plains Anthropologist* 12, no. 35, Memoir 4.

Knight, Douglas A.

1985   "Cosmogony and Order in the Hebrew Tradition." In Robin W. Lovin and Frank E. Reynolds, eds. *Cosmogony and Ethical Order: New Studies in Comparative Ethics.* Chicago: University of Chicago Press.

Kroeber, Alfred L.

1902   *The Arapaho.* Bulletin of the American Museum of Natural History 18.

1907   *Gros Ventre Myths and Tales.* American Museum of Natural History, Anthropological Papers, vol. 1, pt. 3.

Kroeber, Karl

1981   *Traditional Literatures of the American Indian: Texts and Interpretations.* Lincoln: University of Nebraska Press.

Linton, Ralph

1926   "The Origin of the Skidi Pawnee Sacrifice to the Morning Star." *American Anthropologist* 28: 457–66.

Lovelock, James

1979   *Gaia: A New Look at Life on Earth.* New York: Oxford University Press.

Lovin, Robert W., and Frank E. Reynolds

1985   *Cosmogony and Ethical Order: New Studies in Comparative Ethics.* Chicago: University of Chicago Press.

Lowie, Robert H.

1908   "The Test Theme in North American Mythology." *Journal of American Folk-Lore* 21: 91–148.

1909   *The Assiniboine.* American Museum of Natural History, Anthropological Papers, vol. 9, pt. 1.

1913   *Dance Associations of the Eastern Dakota.* American Museum of Natural History, Anthropological Papers, vol. 11, pt. 2.

1915a   *Societies of the Arikara Indians.* American Museum of Natural History, Anthropological Papers, vol. 11, pt. 8.

1915b   *The Sun Dance of the Crow Indians.* American Museum of Natural History, Anthropological Papers, vol. 16, pt. 1.

1918   *Myths and Traditions of the Crow Indians*. American Museum of Natural History, Anthropological Papers, vol. 25, pt. 1.

1922   *The Religion of the Crow Indians*. American Museum of Natural History, Anthropological Papers, vol. 25, pt. 2.

1935   *The Crow Indians*. New York: Farrar and Rinehart.

MacCannell, Dean

1989   *The Tourist: A New Theory of the Leisure Class*. New York: Schocken Books.

Mandelbaum, David G.

1940   *The Plains Cree*. American Museum of Natural History, Anthropological Papers, vol. 37.

Marcus, George E., and Michael M. J. Fischer

1986   *Anthropology as Cultural Critique: An Experimental Moment in the Human Sciences*. Chicago: University of Chicago Press.

Martin, Calvin

1978   *Keepers of the Game: Indian-Animal Relationships and the Fur Trade*. Berkeley: University of California Press.

Maximilian, Alexander Philipp, Prinz von Weid-Neuwied

1906   *Travels in the Interior of North America, 1832–1834*. Vol. 23 of *Early Western Travels, 1748–1846*. Ed. Reuben Gold Thwaites. Cleveland: Arthur H. Clark Company.

McClintock, Walter

1968   *The Old North Trail: Life, Legends and Religion of the Blackfeet Indians*. Lincoln: University of Nebraska Press.

McFague, Sallie

1997   *Super, Natural Christians: How We Should Love Nature*. Minneapolis: Fortress Press.

McGibben, Bill

1989   *The End of Nature*. New York: Random House.

McLean, John

1892   "Blackfoot Mythology." *Journal of American Folk-Lore* 6, no. 22: 165–72.

Melody, Michael Edward

1977   "Maka's Story: A Study of a Lakota Cosmogony." *Journal of American Folklore* 90, no. 356: 149–67.

Merchant, Carolyn

1980   *The Death of Nature: Women, Ecology, and the Scientific Revolution*. San Francisco: Harper and Row.

Mill, John Stuart

1957   *Utilitarianism*. Ed. Oskar Piest. New York: Bobbs-Merrill Company.

Milloy, John S.

1988   *The Plains Cree: Trade, Diplomacy and War, 1790 to 1870*. Manitoba Studies in Native History 4. Winnipeg, Manitoba: University of Manitoba Press.

Momaday, N. Scott

1969   *The Way to Rainy Mountain*. Albuquerque: University of New Mexico Press.

Murie, James R.

1914   *Pawnee Indian Societies*. American Museum of Natural History, Anthropological Papers, vol. 11, pt. 7.

1984   *Ceremonies of the Pawnee*. Ed. Douglas R. Parks. Lincoln: University of Nebraska Press. Originally published as Smithsonian Contributions to Anthropology, no. 21 (1981).

Nelson, Richard K.

1983   *Make Prayers to the Raven: A Koyukon View of the Northern Forest*. Chicago: University of Chicago Press.

Niebuhr, H. Richard

1960   *Radical Monotheism and Western Culture*. New York: Harper and Brothers.

Pepper, George H., and Gilbert L. Wilson

1908   *An Hidatsa Shrine and the Beliefs Respecting It*. Memoirs of the American Anthropological Association, vol. 2, pt. 4.

Peters, Virginia Bergman

1995   *Women of the Earth Lodges: Tribal Life on the Plains*. North Haven, Conn.: Archon Books.

Powers, William K.

1977   *Oglala Religion*. Lincoln: University of Nebraska Press.

Roe, Frank Gilbert

1955   *The Indian and the Horse*. Norman: University of Oklahoma Press.

1970   *The North American Buffalo*. 2nd ed. Toronto: University of Toronto Press.

Sahlins, Marshall

1972   *Stone Age Economics*. New York: Aldine de Gruyter.

Said, Edward

1979   *Orientalism*. New York: Vintage Books.

1994   *Culture and Imperialism*. New York: Vintage Books.

Schlesier, Karl

1987   *The Wolves of Heaven: Cheyenne Shamanism, Ceremonies, and Prehistoric Origins*. Norman: University of Oklahoma Press.

Schutz, Alfred

1967   *Collected Papers I: The Problem of Social Reality*. Ed. Maurice Natanson. The Hague: Martinus Nijhoff.

Schutz, Alfred, and Thomas Luckmann

1973   *The Structures of the Life-World I.* Trans. Richard M. Zaner and H. Tristram Englehardt Jr. Evanston, Ill.: Northwestern University Press.

1989   *The Structures of the Life-World II.* Trans. Richard M. Zaner and David J. Parent. Evanston, Ill.: Northwestern University Press.

Scriver, Bob

1990   *The Blackfeet: Artists of the Northern Plains.* Kansas City: Lowell Press.

Simms, S. C.

1903   *Traditions of the Crows.* Field Columbian Museum, Anthropological Series, Publication 85, vol. 2, pt. 6.

Skinner, Alanson

1914   *Political Organization, Cults, and Ceremonies of the Plains-Ojibway and Plains-Cree Indians.* American Museum of Natural History, Anthropological Papers, vol. 11, pt. 6.

1915a *Societies of the Iowa, Kansa, and Ponca Indians.* American Museum of Natural History, Anthropological Papers, vol. 11, pt. 9.

1915b *Social Life and Ceremonial Bundles of the Menomini Indians.* American Museum of Natural History, Anthropological Papers, vol. 13, pt. 1.

Speck, Frank G.

1935   *Naskapi.* Norman: University of Oklahoma Press.

Spier, Leslie

1921   *The Sun Dance of the Plains Indians: Its Development and Diffusion.* American Museum of Natural History, Anthropological Papers, vol. 16, pt. 7.

Stewart, Frank Henderson

1977   *Fundamentals of Age-Group Systems.* New York: Academic Press.

Swann, Brian

1983   *Smoothing the Ground: Essays on Native American Oral Literature.* Berkeley: University of California Press.

Tanner, Adrian

1979   *Bringing Home Animals: Religious Ideology and Mode of Production of the Mistassini Cree Hunters.* New York: St. Martin's Press.

Thomas, Lewis

1974   *The Lives of a Cell.* New York: Viking Press.

Uhlenbeck, C. C.

1912   *Original Blackfoot Texts from the Southern Piegans Blackfoot Reservation Teton County Montana.* Verhandelingen der Koninklijke Akademie van Wetenschappen. Afdeeling Letterkunde, Nieuwe Reeks, vol. 12, pt. 1. Amsterdam: Johannes Muller.

1913   *New Series of Blackfoot Texts from the Southern Piegans Blackfoot Reservation Teton County Montana*. Verhandelingen der Koninklijke Akademie van Wetenschappen. Afdeeling Letterkunde, Nieuwe Reeks, vol. 13, pt. 1. Amsterdam: Johannes Muller.

Uhlenbeck, C. C., and R. H. Van Gulik

1934   *A Blackfoot-English Vocabulary*. Verhandelingen der Koninklijke Akademie van Wetenschappen te Amsterdam. Afdeeling Letterkunde, Nieuwe Reeks, vol. 33, pt. 2.

Vansina, Jan

1965   *Oral Tradition: A Study in Historical Methodology*. Chicago: Aldine Publishing Company.

1985   *Oral Tradition as History*. Madison: University of Wisconsin Press.

Walker, James R.

1905   "Sioux Games I." *Journal of American Folk-Lore* 18: 277–90.

1906   "Sioux Games II." *Journal of American Folk-Lore* 19: 29–36.

1917   *The Sun Dance and Other Ceremonies of the Oglala Division of the Teton Dakota*. American Museum of Natural History, Anthropological Papers, vol. 16, pt. 2.

1982a   *Lakota Society*. Ed. Raymond J. DeMallie. Lincoln: University of Nebraska Press.

1982b   *Lakota Belief and Ritual*. Ed. Raymond J. DeMallie and Elaine A. Jahner. Lincoln: University of Nebraska Press.

1983   *Lakota Myth*. Ed. Elaine A. Jahner. Lincoln: University of Nebraska Press.

Wallis, Wilson D.

1923   "Beliefs and Tales of the Canadian Dakota." *Journal of American Folk-Lore* 36: 36–101.

White, Lynn Jr.

1967   "The Historical Roots of Our Ecologic Crisis." *Science* 155: 1203–7.

Wildschut, William

1960   *Crow Indian Medicine Bundles*. Ed. John C. Ewers. Contributions from the Museum of the American Indian Heye Foundation 17.

Wilson, Gilbert Livingston

1928   *Hidatsa Eagle Trapping*. American Museum of Natural History, Anthropological Papers, vol. 30, pt. 4.

Wissler, Clark

1908   "Ethnographical Problems of the Missouri Saskatchewan Area." *American Anthropologist* 10: 197–207.

1910   *Material Culture of the Blackfoot Indians*. American Museum of Natural History, Anthropological Papers, vol. 5, pt. 1.

1911   *The Social Life of the Blackfoot Indians.* American Museum of Natural History, Anthropological Papers, vol. 7, pt. 1.

1912   *Ceremonial Bundles of the Blackfoot Indians.* American Museum of Natural History, Anthropological Papers, vol. 7, pt. 2.

1913   *Societies and Dance Associations of the Blackfoot Indians.* American Museum of Natural History, Anthropological Papers, vol. 11, pt. 4.

1916   *Societies of the Plains Indians.* American Museum of Natural History, Anthropological Papers, vol. 11.

1918   *The Sundance of the Blackfoot Indians.* American Museum of Natural History, Anthropological Papers, vol. 16, pt. 3.

1921   *Sun Dance of the Plains Indians.* American Museum of Natural History, Anthropological Papers, vol. 16.

1946   *Star Legends among the American Indians.* Science Guide no. 91. New York: American Museum of Natural History.

Wissler, Clark, and D. C. Duvall

1908   *Mythology of the Blackfoot Indians.* American Museum of Natural History, Anthropological Papers, vol. 2, pt. 1.

index

about the author

Howard L. Harrod is Oberlin Alumni Professor of Social Ethics and Sociology of Religion and Professor of Religious Studies at Vanderbilt University, where he has taught since 1968. His research and teaching focus on the sociology of religion and Native American religions on the Northern Plains. He is the author of four books and numerous articles. The University of Oklahoma, in its Civilization of the American Indian Series, published his first book, *Mission among the Blackfeet* (1971; reissued 1999). *The Human Center: Moral Agency in the Social World,* a book reflecting his interests in phenomenological sociology, was published by Fortress Press in 1981. Two studies on Northern Plains religions have been published by the University of Arizona Press: *Renewing the World: Plains Indian Religion and Morality* (1987) and *Becoming and Remaining a People: Native American Religions on the Northern Plains* (1995). Research for these books was supported by grants from the American Council of Learned Societies and the Rockefeller Foundation. This book is a continuation of his work on Northern Plains religious and moral traditions.